THE SOFT CIRCLE

© 2025 Rebecca Park. All rights reserved.

No part of this book may be reproduced in any form without written permission from the publisher, except for brief quotations in reviews or articles.

This book is intended for educational and informational purposes only and is not a substitute for professional medical, psychological, legal, or financial advice. Always seek the guidance of a qualified professional with any questions you may have regarding a medical or mental health condition.

ISBN (paperback): [978-1-7644223-0-7]
ISBN (ebook): [978-1-7644223-1-4]

ISBN (Hardback): [978-1-7644223-2-1]

Cover design: [Rebecca Park]

Illustrations: [Rebeeca Park]

Contents

Epigraph	V
Author's Note	VI
PART I - Wound	1
1. The Child Who Learned to Survive	3
2. The Nervous System Remembers	11
3. The Mask I Learned to Wear	18
4. Love, Attachment, and Fear	24
5. The Family Blueprint: How We Inherit Wounds We Don't Remember	30
PART II - The Breaking Open	44
6. The Pattern Breaking Moment	45
7. The Body Speaks What the Mind Cannot	51
8. Meeting the Shadow Self	58
9. The Soul's View of Suffering	65
PART III The Returning	72
10. Safety in the Body	73
11. Speaking to Inner Child	78
12. Healing Intimacy	83
13. Love After Awakening	106
PART IV Integration	120
14. Rituals for a Soft Life	121
15. HEALING IS NOT LINEAR	129

16.	YOU ARE BECOMING WHOLE	138
17.	Returning to Innocence: Aging as a Sacred Homecoming	150
Epilogue — The Gentle Doorway		161

Epigraph

"You do not heal by becoming someone new.

You heal by returning to who you've always been."

Author's Note

This book was not written from a mountaintop.

It was written from a human life — from moments of breaking, returning, learning, forgetting, and trying again. None of these chapters come from perfection. They come from curiosity, from self-education, from countless nights reading psychology, neuroscience, trauma research, and the many spiritual traditions that have shaped my understanding of what it means to heal.

I am not a therapist, a scientist, or a guru.

I am simply someone who wants to understand why we suffer, why we repeat patterns that hurt us, and how we can come home to ourselves after years — sometimes decades — of living in survival mode. Everything in these pages is something I have lived through, learned through, or walked through with someone I love.

Manly — the ocean, the pines, the people I've met here — became the quiet ground that helped me begin writing. Life has been my teacher. Every human I've crossed paths with, every story shared with me, every joy and wound I've witnessed, became part of this book. I learned that healing is not a destination but a relationship with yourself, one you return to again and again.

If these words find you at a tender moment, I hope they remind you that nothing about you is broken beyond repair. You are simply carrying old protections, old stories,

AUTHOR'S NOTE

old versions of yourself that once kept you safe. You can learn to put them down slowly, gently, in your own time.

Thank you for letting me walk with you for a few chapters of your life.

May these pages offer softness where you've been hard on yourself, understanding where there has been confusion, and hope where something inside you grew tired.

Most of all, I hope this book helps you return — patiently, bravely — to yourself.

With love,

Rebecca

***

PART I - Wound

I grew around a hurt, I never learned to name.

It lived in my body quietly, shaping my breath, my choices,

the way I held myself

when no one was watching.

I carried it so long

it began to feel like identity— as if the ache

was the same thing

as "me."

But underneath the layers, beneath the practiced strength

and the quiet pretending,

my true self, never disappeared.

She simply lived hidden, waiting for the day

I would look inward, instead of away.

Now I am learning that the wound

is not who I am—

it is only the place where I first learned

to survive.

And healing is remembering

the self that existed

before the pain

taught me to hide.

-Author

Chapter 1
The Child Who Learned to Survive

None of us arrives in this world by choice. We do not choose our parents, our environment, or the emotional climate we are born into. We enter life unguarded, open, and impressionable. Our early world teaches us who we are, how to love, how to endure, and how to stay safe long before we have language to understand any of it. A human baby is one of the most dependent living beings. A newborn cannot walk, cannot feed itself, cannot calm itself, and cannot make meaning of what it feels. It depends entirely on the environment around it.

Not only for physical survival, but for emotional survival. Before we know words, we learn the world through sensation.

> The rhythm of a parent's breathing.
> The softness or sharpness of a tone.
> The warmth or absence of touch.
> The atmosphere inside the home.
> The speed at which someone moves.
> How people look when they are angry.
> How they look just before they become angry.

Our body begins learning long before we think.

How Safety Is Learned

The emotional brain, called the limbic system, develops early. It is responsible for detecting danger and seeking connection. The thinking brain, the prefrontal cortex, which allows reasoning and emotional regulation, develops much later, finishing around age twenty five.

This means a child does not understand their environment. They *feel* it.

They sense patterns, tone, tension, closeness, distance.

So when something overwhelming or confusing happens, the child does not say:

"This is unhealthy."

The child says:

"This must be normal."

"This must be love."

"This must be what people are like."

And most importantly:

"This is who I must become to survive here."

Identity begins here, not from desire or self-expression, but from adaptation.

We learn to:

Stay quiet to avoid conflict

Stay small so we are not noticed

Stay cheerful so no one asks questions

Stay strong so no one sees our fear

Work hard to earn approval

Withdraw to avoid disappointment

These are not personality traits.

They are survival strategies written directly into our nervous system.

The Nervous System Remembers

In the book *The Body Keeps the Score*, trauma specialist Dr. Bessel van der Kolk explains that emotional experiences are stored in the body. Even when the mind does not recall details, the body remembers the state it had to enter to survive.

The child who had to stay quiet to keep peace often becomes the adult who struggles to speak their needs.

The child who had to become strong becomes the adult who cannot allow themselves to be held.

The child who had to stay invisible becomes the adult who feels replaced, overlooked, or easily abandoned.

The child who had to walk on eggshells learns to read every room before they even enter it.

This happens outside conscious awareness.
The body responds faster than thought.

Walking on Eggshells: How Hypervigilance Begins

When home feels unpredictable, the nervous system learns to scan constantly. Listening for footsteps. Checking tone. Watching eyes. Noticing silence. Feeling the air change.

This becomes automatic.

The heart learns to anticipate danger even when there is none.
The breath shortens before the mind knows why.
The stomach tightens without a clear reason.
The jaw holds tension year after year.

This is not anxiety.
This is a body that once needed to be alert in order to survive.

Hypervigilance is not a flaw.
It is expertise.

You became excellent at noticing what others ignore.

How the Brain Stores Emotional Memory

The amygdala is responsible for recognizing threats.
It learns quickly and remembers strongly.

The prefrontal cortex is responsible for understanding context.
It learns slowly and remembers softly.
So when something painful happens in childhood:
The body remembers the emotion.

The mind does not yet understand the cause.

This is why in adulthood:

A raised voice feels like danger.

Silence feels like abandonment.

Love feels both safe and unsafe.

Closeness feels desired and frightening at the same time.

Your reaction is not about the present moment.
It is a memory in the nervous system activating to protect you.

The Vagus Nerve and the Body's Response
The vagus nerve is the communication line between the brain and body. It decides whether we are in:
Safety
Alert
Collapse
Shut down

When the vagus nerve senses safety, the body softens. Breath slows. Muscles release. Eyes relax.
When it senses potential danger, the body prepares to protect. Breath shortens. Muscles tighten. Vision narrows. Thoughts become defensive or fuzzy.

This happens before thought.
Before logic.
Before reflection.

This is why healing cannot happen by forcing yourself to "think differently."
The body must first learn that it is safe now.

Common Emotional Childhood Environments

Pain is not always dramatic.
Pain often comes quietly.

Here are six emotional climates many people grew up in. You may recognize more than one.

1. The Chaotic Home

Emotions change quickly. There is unpredictability. The child learns to watch constantly.

Adult pattern: anxiety, scanning, difficulty resting.

2. The Emotionally Quiet Home

Everything appears calm, but feelings are unspoken. The child learns to suppress emotion.

Adult pattern: numbness, difficulty identifying needs, a sense of emptiness.

3. The Performance Home

Love is earned through achievement. Mistakes feel dangerous.

Adult pattern: perfectionism, self-criticism, never feeling enough.

4. The Caretaking Home

The child becomes an emotional adult. They soothe others to maintain stability.

Adult pattern: people-pleasing, exhaustion, inability to receive support.

5. The Enmeshed Home

Closeness exists, but identity is blurred. The child never learns where they end and others begin.

Adult pattern: confusion in boundaries and relationships.

6. The Hyper-Independent Home

Feelings are dismissed. Strength is praised. Vulnerability is viewed as weakness.

Adult pattern: self-reliance to the point of loneliness.

Not all homes are visibly harmful.
Some are simply emotionally unskilled.

Pain does not require violence to take root.
Pain requires only silence where understanding should be.

A Personal Memory (Soft, Symbolic)

I learned how to be the bright one. The one who laughed easily. The one who created warmth in cold rooms. I knew how to make others feel safe even when I did not feel safe myself. I did not want anyone to worry. I did not want to be seen as struggling. I learned early how to place my sadness behind my back and offer only light to the world.

You may have your own version of this.
The child who learned to become small.
The child who learned to become strong.
The child who became responsible.
The child who became invisible.
The child who became everything others needed.

We wore these identities like second skin.
So well that we forgot there was someone underneath.

Adult Life, Same Patterns, New Cost

Patterns that protected us in childhood become limitations in adulthood.
The silence that once kept peace becomes loneliness.
The strength that once protected us becomes isolation.
The humor that once softened pain becomes avoidance.
The independence that once kept us safe becomes disconnected.

This is not failure.
This is what survival looks like when it has not yet learned how to rest.

Healing Begins With Recognition

Healing does not begin with forcing yourself to change.
Healing begins when you recognize:

"I adapted to survive."

Not:

"I am broken."
"I am wrong."

"I am too much."
"I am not enough."
But:
"I learned this."
"And I can learn something new."
You are not trying to become someone new.
You are remembering who you were before fear made you hide.
You are not undoing yourself.
You are returning to yourself.

Spiritual Meaning:

You were born whole, and what you learned later were layers of protection. Healing is not about becoming someone new. It is remembering who you were before fear taught you to hide.

Quote:

"You did not become this way because you were weak. You became this way because you were wise."

Healing Practice:

Place one hand on your heart.
Take a slow breath in.
Take a slow breath out.
Say quietly to yourself:
"I survived. Now I am learning how to live."

THE SOFT CIRCLE

Chapter 2
The Nervous System Remembers

There are moments when your body speaks louder than your thoughts. You might be in a calm conversation, in the presence of someone you care for, or sitting alone in a quiet room, and suddenly something inside you shifts. Your heart starts to beat faster. Your stomach tightens. Your breath becomes short. Your mind begins to sharpen or disappear. You may not understand why, but the reaction feels immediate and overwhelming.

This is not irrational.

This is the nervous system remembering something you had to survive.

Your nervous system learned how to read the world long before you could speak. Before you formed conscious memories. Before language. Before you learned the meaning of your own feelings.

As a child, your first understanding of the world came through sensation: the warmth or coldness of someone's presence, the tone of a voice, the heaviness in a room, the way the air changed when someone walked in angry or unpredictable. None of this required words. Your body recorded all of it.

Long before you had a story about your life, your body had a story about safety.

This is why the body reacts faster than the mind.
The body learned its lessons earlier.

The Body Reacts Before You Can Think

The nervous system scans every moment for signals of safety or threat. This happens automatically and continuously. You do not choose it. You do not control it. You do not think your way through it. It happens in the background, like a silent radar searching the emotional environment.

This process is called neuroception.
It is not thinking.
It is sensing.

Neuroscience researcher Dr. Andrew Huberman explains that the nervous system reads the smallest emotional cues: a shift in someone's tone, how they breathe before they respond, tension in their shoulders, the energy of a room that feels heavier today than yesterday. These signals are interpreted faster than conscious thought.

By the time your mind tries to make sense of what is happening, your body has already decided how to react.

This is why your reaction appears sudden.
It was not sudden.
It was learned.

Your body is not responding to the moment itself.
Your body is responding to what the moment resembles.

When something in the present feels similar to something once overwhelming, frightening, or unsafe, the nervous system reacts as if the past is happening again.

You may not remember the event.
You remember the feeling.

The Vagus Nerve and the Story of Safety

The vagus nerve is the communication channel between your brain and your body. It influences your breathing, digestion, heart rate, emotional presence, facial expression, and tone of voice. It is one of the main pathways through which the body decides whether it is safe to relax or whether it needs to defend itself.

When the vagus nerve senses safety, your body softens. Your breath deepens. Your awareness expands. You feel grounded in the moment. You feel like yourself.

When the vagus nerve senses possible danger, even subtle danger, your muscles tighten, your breath becomes shallow, and your thoughts shift toward protection. The world begins to feel sharper. Your awareness narrows. You may either react, withdraw, freeze, or work to keep the peace.

This is the same instinct that kept you alive as a child. The body learned to anticipate danger before it arrived. It learned to read emotional climates the way animals read changing weather.

Your nervous system became your guardian before you ever knew danger existed.

The problem is not the body.

The problem is that no one ever told the body that the danger is over.

The Past Is Stored as Sensation

Dr. Bruce D. Perry, in the book *What Happened to You?*, explains that overwhelming experiences are not stored as stories. They are stored as states. Meaning: the body keeps the memory as sensation.

This is why you may feel triggered without knowing why.

The body is not reacting to the present.

The body is reacting to something *you once survived*.

A familiar tone of voice.

A certain kind of silence.

A shift in someone's expression.

A moment where you feel unseen.

A situation where connection feels uncertain.

These moments echo something earlier.

The body does not forget what it had to protect you from.

Automatic Survival Responses

When the body perceives a threat, it chooses the survival response it learned first and practiced most. This may show up as:

Fight: Defending, arguing, reacting intensely.

Flight: Leaving, avoiding, staying busy, disappearing.

Freeze: Going numb, losing words, shutting down.

Fawn: Trying to keep the peace, pleasing to avoid conflict.

These are not personality traits.
They are adaptive strategies.
You did not choose them.
They formed in the absence of choice.
They protected you when you did not have power.
Now they appear even when you are safe because your body does not yet know the difference.

The Body Will Not Let Go Until It Feels Safe
You cannot think your way out of survival mode.
You cannot argue with your reactions.
You cannot force your body into calmness.
The nervous system does not respond to logic.
It responds to experience.
Healing requires showing the body safety, not talking about safety.
The body needs to experience calm repeatedly to believe that it is allowed to put its guard down.
This is not a quick process.
It is not linear.
It is not something you accomplish in a week of meditation or one breakthrough conversation.
It is learned through slow, real, physical experience.

Breath as the First Doorway Back to the Body
The most direct way to signal safety to the nervous system is through breath.
The Softened Exhale;
Inhale gently through the nose for four seconds.
Exhale slowly through the mouth for six seconds.

The longer exhale activates the vagus nerve and tells the body:
You can soften now.

The Hum Exhale;

Inhale through the nose.

Exhale with a quiet hum vibrating in your chest.

This vibration helps regulate the heart rhythm and signals emotional safety.

Box Breathing;

Inhale for four seconds.

Hold for four seconds.

Exhale for four seconds.

Hold again for four seconds.

Repeat.

This steady pattern is used in trauma recovery to re-establish presence.

These are not ways to control your emotions.

These are ways to communicate with your nervous system.

You are not trying to silence your body.

You are trying to reassure it.

The body does not need discipline.

The body needs acknowledgment.

Listening Instead of Correcting

There is nothing wrong with you for reacting the way you do.

Your nervous system adapted to the emotional environment it grew in. It learned to protect you in the only ways it could. It is doing what it was trained to do.

Healing begins with recognition, not correction.

Instead of asking

"What is wrong with me?"

try asking

"What is my body trying to protect me from?"

The answer is always something real.

A Real Moment

You are having a conversation with someone you love. The conversation is normal, maybe even pleasant. Then something shifts. Their tone changes slightly. Their attention feels different. There is a tiny interruption in closeness.

Your body reacts.

You tense.

You withdraw or cling.

You speak too quickly or say nothing at all.

Your mind may say:

"This is small. I should not feel this way."

But your body remembers a different story:

"When closeness shifts, abandonment follows."

Your reaction is not excessive.

Your body is responding to a memory it never got to resolve.

This Is Not Your Fault

You are not dramatic.

You are not weak.

You are not broken.

Your nervous system simply learned how to survive.

Now we teach it how to live.

Spiritual Meaning:

The body reacts first because it once had to protect you before you had words or understanding. Healing is the slow, gentle process of reminding the body that it no longer needs to guard every moment. You are not in the past anymore.

Quote:

"Your reaction is not who you are. It is where you have been."

Healing Practice:

Place one hand on your heart.

Breathe in slowly through your nose.

Exhale gently through your mouth.

Repeat six times.

Do not try to change the feeling.

Simply be present with it.
Your body is remembering you.

Chapter 3
The Mask I Learned to Wear

I did not grow up in a home where safety was consistent. I learned early that the emotional weather could change without warning. My father's addiction shaped the atmosphere of the house. I became familiar with small signals most children never have to notice. The sound of footsteps. The rhythm of breathing. The tone behind a door opening. I paid attention because my body needed to know what version of him would walk into the room. I was not learning out of curiosity. I was learning to survive.

My mother was trying to survive too, in the only ways she could. There were moments she had to leave to protect herself. And so I was there with my younger brother, trying to make the world make sense while it never stood still. There was no space to collapse. No room to express fear. No time to feel.

There was always the next morning.
School did not wait for healing.
Life did not pause because my home was falling apart.

So I learned to perform being okay.

The world measures how well a child can function, not how deeply they are in pain. So I became the funny one. Humour became my shield. If I could make others laugh, then no one would look too closely. If I stayed bright and quick and playful, people would not sense the heaviness I carried.

On the outside, I was light.
On the inside, I was tired.

Humour gave me a way to stay in the world without showing my wounds.

I know now that many children in unstable homes develop similar masks. When a parent's emotional world is unpredictable, the child must adjust themselves constantly to prevent chaos. This is not personality. This is survival.

Dr. Lindsay Gibson, in *Adult Children of Emotionally Immature Parents*, explains that when a parent's emotional needs overshadow the child's, the child becomes the emotional regulator of the household. They learn to soothe, entertain, accommodate, or disappear to prevent conflict. They learn that stability depends on them.

People call this being "a people-pleaser."
But people-pleasing is not a desire to be nice.
It is a survival strategy.

If I keep you calm, I stay safe.
If I keep you happy, I will not be harmed.
If I stay agreeable, I will not be abandoned.

Not every child becomes the funny one.
But every child learns *something* that helps them survive.

Some learn to be strong, never asking for help.
Some learn to excel, believing perfection prevents chaos.
Some learn to disappear, believing invisibility is safer than presence.
Some become caregivers, stepping into emotional adulthood long before they were ready.

Even as adults, these masks remain.
Not because we want them.
But because they once worked.

The mask is not the enemy.
The mask is the proof of how intelligent your survival was.

The trouble begins when the mask becomes so familiar that you forget there is someone underneath.

How the Mask Becomes Identity

The brain is shaped by repetition. Whatever pattern kept you safe becomes wired as normal. The nervous system does not distinguish between survival patterns and authentic self. It only recognizes what worked.

If humour kept you from being hurt, your body will use humour automatically.
If silence protected you, your body will shut down before you speak.
If strength kept the world at a distance, your body will resist vulnerability without your permission.

These patterns do not ask for your input.
They activate themselves.

This is why intimacy can feel threatening even when you desire it.
Closeness asks you to remove the protection that once kept you alive.

Your body remembers what exposure once cost you.

How the Mask Shows Up in Adult Life

Later in life, the mask can create confusion.
People may think you are confident, self-assured, independent, composed, funny, easy, or strong.
But those traits may be armor.

You may be physically close to others, while emotionally hidden.
You may be loved by many, but truly known by no one.

You may feel like you are in the room but behind glass.

This is not because you do not want a connection.
It is because connection once felt dangerous.

Your body is not resisting love.
Your body is remembering the past.

When the Mask Starts to Crack

There comes a moment where the mask becomes too heavy.
Not because you failed.
But because you outgrew survival.

This usually happens in relationships.

Someone gets close enough to see past the surface.

And your first impulse is either to pull away, make a joke, shut down, or change the subject.

Not because you do not care.

But because you care so much that the risk becomes overwhelming.

To let someone in means letting someone touch the places that were once injured.

And that requires time.

Gentleness.

Patience.

Safety.

Healing Is Not Ripping the Mask Off

You do not need to "stop being the funny one."

You do not need to stop being strong, or capable, or calm.

These parts of you are real.

They are skilled.

They are beautiful.

We are not removing anything.

We are learning to soften.

To loosen the grip.

To breathe into the places we once held tightly.

To let one person in at a time.

To tell the truth slowly.

To speak before the performance begins.

To stay when the impulse is to disappear.

Healing is the quiet return to the self you were before protection became necessary.

Not all at once.

Not dramatically.

Just one breath more open than yesterday.

Spiritual Meaning:

The mask you learned was love, not weakness. It was your body protecting your heart when the world could not. Healing is remembering that safety can now exist from within.

Quote:

"The mask kept me safe when safety was not available. Now I am learning who I am without it."

Healing Practice:

Write one sentence that begins with:

"If I did not need to perform right now, I would say…"

Do not edit.

Do not justify.

Do not explain.

Just allow what appears to be seen.

Chapter 4
Love, Attachment, and Fear

Love is not only emotional. It is biological, chemical, nervous-system based. When we form a connection with someone, the brain releases dopamine, oxytocin, and vasopressin, chemicals that create desire, bonding, and trust. At the same time, the amygdala, the part of the brain that scans for emotional danger, remains alert. If your early experiences with love or care were inconsistent, overwhelming, or unpredictable, these two systems begin to conflict with each other. Love becomes something you want deeply but also something your body feels it must protect you from.

This is why you can long for closeness while feeling the urge to withdraw the moment closeness arrives. Your body remembers what your mind cannot always explain.

The nervous system learned how to approach and defend at the same time.

Neuroscientist Andrew Huberman explains that the nervous system evaluates safety long before conscious thought. When someone moves closer to you emotionally, your body does not decide based on the present moment alone. It responds based on what closeness once meant. The signal does not come from memory. It comes from sensation. It comes from the body.

If closeness once led to chaos, abandonment, confusion, or emotional responsibility, then closeness in adulthood will activate both longing and fear. One part of you wants to move forward. Another part of you is already stepping back.

You are not confused.

Your nervous system is trying to keep you safe while letting you love.

Both are real.

Love as Co-Regulation

Science and spirituality describe the same experience of love in different languages.

Science says love is co-regulation.

Two nervous systems communicating safety.

You feel it when someone's voice is gentle, when their presence is steady, when they breathe in a calm rhythm, when their face softens instead of tensing. You may not consciously notice these things, but your body does. Your heart rate slows. Your muscles release. The mind stops scanning the environment. Your entire system shifts from survival to presence.

This is the biology of safety.

Spirituality describes love as the experience of being seen without needing to perform or adjust yourself. It is the quiet awareness that there is space for you to exist exactly as you are.

Science calls this secure attachment.

Spirituality calls this home.

When Early Love Was Inconsistent

Attachment theory explains that the nervous system learns love from our earliest relationships. In the book *Attached* by Amir Levine and Rachel Heller, secure attachment forms when care is reliable, consistent, emotionally available, and attuned. The child learns:

"I can reach for connection and it will be met."

But when a caregiver is warm in one moment and overwhelmed, distant, distracted, angry, emotionally shut down, or unpredictable in the next, the child receives two messages:

"Love feels good," and

"Love is dangerous."

The nervous system holds both.

This is how the push-and-pull dynamic develops in adulthood.

The anxious part reaches for closeness to avoid being left.

The avoidant part pulls back to avoid being hurt.

Both parts are intelligent.

Both formed to protect the heart.

When You Learn to Perform for Love

In many emotionally inconsistent households, the child becomes responsible for the emotional climate of the home. They learn to adjust themselves to keep peace. They learn to soothe, manage, predict, and monitor the parent's emotional state. Love becomes work.

In *Adult Children of Emotionally Immature Parents*, Dr. Lindsay Gibson explains that this teaches the child:

"Love is something I have to maintain."

Not:

"Love is where I rest."

The nervous system does not forget this.

It simply carries it into adult relationships.

You may long for intimacy yet feel overwhelmed when it arrives.

You may crave reassurance but freeze when someone offers it.

You may desire closeness but find peace uncomfortable.

You may feel safest when love is just slightly out of reach.

This is not because you do not want love.

It is because to your body, love has always required work.

Resting in connection feels foreign.

Receiving care feels exposing.

Being seen feels like a risk.

Your body is not resisting love.

Your body is resisting what love used to cost you.

The Body Remembers Love and Loss in the Same Language

Oxytocin, the bonding chemical, is supposed to make connections feel good.

But oxytocin also heightens sensitivity to loss.

This means:

The more someone matters to you,

the stronger your nervous system reacts when connection feels uncertain.

This is why the person you care about most is also the person who can trigger the deepest fear, longing, defensiveness, or withdrawal.

Love is both healing and activating.

Fear is Not the Opposite of Love

Fear does not mean the relationship is wrong.

Fear means the relationship touches a wound.

Fear appears in the exact place the heart is trying to open.

So the work is not to eliminate fear.

The work is to remain present while fear rises.

The moment the breath shortens is the doorway.

The moment the chest tightens is the doorway.

The moment you want to run, shut down, cling, or control is the doorway.

This is where the younger self is speaking.

This is where the body remembers.

This is where healing happens.

Not in thinking differently.

Not in trying harder.

But in staying with yourself while staying in connection.

Love becomes possible when you do not leave yourself to keep the relationship, and you do not leave the relationship to keep yourself.

You stay with both.

This is what healing love looks like:

Slow.

Steady.

Present.

Breath-based.

Unrushed.

Without performance.

Without collapse.

Healing Attachment in the Body

To heal attachment wounds, the goal is not to trust others faster.
The goal is to trust yourself to stay with your own experience.

When your body reacts, pause.
Place your hand on your chest.
Breathe once slowly.
Ask gently inside:

"What part of me is trying to be protected right now?"

You are not fixing the reaction.
You are acknowledging the child who still believes closeness is dangerous.

You are becoming the adult your younger self needed.
This is how love becomes safe.

Spiritual Meaning:

Love begins to feel safe when your heart learns that it does not need to disappear to be loved. The fear is not a sign that love is wrong. The fear is the doorway back to yourself.

Quote:

"I reach for connection and I pull away because both the love and the fear are real, and I am learning how to stay with myself through both."

Healing Practice:

When you feel yourself withdrawing or chasing, pause.
Place your hand on your chest.
Breathe in through your nose and out through your mouth once.
Then ask softly:

"What is the younger part of me needing right now?"

Do not solve.
Just listen.

Chapter 5
The Family Blueprint: How We Inherit Wounds We Don't Remember

5.1— The Invisible Curriculum: What Children Learn Without Words

Every child arrives like a seed—intact, whole, carrying everything needed to grow. And the family becomes the soil. The home becomes the garden. The environment becomes the climate in which this tiny nervous system learns what life is, what love feels like, and what it must do to stay safe.

Children do not learn through language first. They learn through vibration, tone, rhythm, and atmosphere. Long before they understand words, they understand the emotional weather around them. A baby does not know the meaning of "anxiety," but it feels the quickness in a parent's breath. A toddler cannot define "depression," but it recognizes when a room feels dim and heavy. A child cannot explain "avoidance," but it senses when a parent's body stiffens in silence.

Children are sponges. They absorb emotional reality long before cognitive reality.

They learn the world by feeling it.

This is the invisible curriculum.
It teaches without speaking.
It shapes without permission.
It forms the blueprint long before the mind forms memory.

If a parent is calm, the child learns that life is navigable. If a parent is chronically overwhelmed, the child learns the world is unpredictable. If a parent is anxious, the child's nervous system learns to scan for danger even when no threat is present. If a parent is disconnected or depressed, the child may learn to quiet their needs, to take up less space, to tiptoe emotionally through their early years.

And none of this is the parent's fault. They too were once seeds in another garden, shaped by an older curriculum they did not choose.

Modern neuroscience shows that infants regulate their nervous systems through their caregivers. Stephen Porges, known for Polyvagal Theory, calls this *co-regulation*: the way a child's body calibrates safety through the body of the adult caring for them.

This means a child does not only receive love.
A child receives the *nervous system* of the parent.

Their stress becomes the child's baseline.
Their calm becomes the child's home.
Their unresolved wounds become the child's invisible inheritance.

In developmental psychology, this is called emotional imprinting. In epigenetics, it is known as intergenerational transmission — the way trauma, stress responses, and emotional patterns pass down through generations not only through behavior but even through biology.

Mark Wolynn's book *It Didn't Start With You* describes this beautifully: that we often carry feelings, fears, and patterns that do not originate inside our lifetime, but inside the unhealed stories of the people who came before us.

Picture a child who grows up in a home where both parents are overwhelmed. Even if those parents love deeply, their nervous system remains in survival mode. The child feels it. Not in words, but in the tightening of the air. The unspoken rules. The emotional climate. The invisible lessons.

This child learns that vigilance is normal.
That tension is familiar.
That calm is rare and therefore suspicious.

That emotional closeness feels unstable.
That expressing needs could burden someone already drowning.

This is the silent curriculum that shapes a person without ever appearing in the conscious mind.

A child enters life like a blank page — a white board — and the world begins writing. Every gesture becomes grammar. Every silence becomes punctuation. Every emotional moment becomes a line in the story the nervous system learns to tell.

As adults, we often mistake this curriculum for our personality:

"I am anxious."
"I am an avoidant."
"I don't trust easily."
"I get overwhelmed quickly."
"I feel too much."
"I shut down without knowing why."

But these are not personality traits.
They are survival lessons, learned early, practiced daily, and stored deep in the body.

The invisible curriculum is powerful because it is unconscious. It is not taught; it is absorbed. It is not explained; it is felt. It does not ask permission; it simply becomes the language through which we understand the world.

Yet the beauty is this: the curriculum is not permanent.

The nervous system can relearn.
Patterns can be rewritten.
The body can discover new meanings.
The child within us can receive the nurturing they missed.
The garden can be re-planted.

Awareness begins the rewriting.
Compassion continues it.
Practice completes it.

What we inherited unconsciously, we can transform consciously.

And what began in the soil does not have to define the entire forest that grows from it.

5.2 — How Parents Pass Down Unprocessed Pain

(When Love and Hurt Become One Language)

Every family teaches a child something long before words or lessons ever appear.
Not through instructions, but through atmosphere.
Children don't learn emotional life from explanations —
they learn it from the feeling of being around their caregivers.

A child reads the home the way a seed reads soil.
Whatever is in the soil — warmth, tension, chaos, tenderness, silence, fear —
The seed grows around it.

Even if a parent never explains their stress or speaks about their past, the child still absorbs the emotional climate.
Not because something is wrong with the child —
but because children are designed to tune themselves to the people who keep them alive.

This is how unprocessed pain travels from one generation to the next:
quietly, automatically, and without anyone meaning harm.

Not Genetics — But How Experience Leaves Traces

Modern science now shows that high stress, unresolved trauma, and chronic emotional strain can leave chemical marks on genes — a field known as epigenetics.

But unlike heavier science chapters you've read before, let's keep this simple:

Epigenetics means:
your body remembers what your parents survived.

Not as a story,
but as sensitivity.

A parent who lived in fear may unconsciously pass down a nervous system that reacts more quickly.
A parent who survived neglect may pass down patterns of emotional self-protection.
A parent who grew up walking on eggshells may raise a child who becomes careful without knowing why.

This is not destiny —
It's a starting point.

When Parents Carry Pain They Haven't Worked Through

Parents never set out to wound their children.
Most parents love their kids fiercely.
But love alone does not erase a parent's history.

A parent who never learned to feel safe may struggle to give safety.
A parent who never received emotional support may not know how to attune.
A parent who grew up overwhelmed may shut down when the child has big feelings.
A parent who learned to stay quiet may become frightened when their child expresses strong emotion.

These reactions are not intentional —
They are reflexes from the parent's own past.

Children don't see the past.
They only see themselves reflected in the parent's face.

So the child learns:

"My feelings are too much."

"I need to be quiet so no one gets upset."

"Love means working hard for attention."

"Closeness feels unpredictable."

"It's safer to take care of others than myself."

These are not personality traits.
They are adaptations.

When Love and Pain Mix Together

If a child grows up in an environment where the same person who gives love also creates fear, distance, or unpredictability, the child's nervous system becomes confused.

Not because the parent is bad —
but because unresolved pain leaks into connection.

What this creates is not simply "insecure attachment."
It's something deeper and more confusing:

The child learns that love requires self-protection.

This wiring follows them into adulthood:
They may choose partners who feel familiar rather than healthy.

They may pull away when things become intimate.

They may mistake intensity for care.

They may stay in relationships that hurt, because challenge feels normal.

Or they may reject good love because safety feels foreign.

This is not a conscious choice —
It is a nervous system repeating what it learned early.

How Emotional Patterns Get Recycled

A powerful truth from family-systems psychology:
We don't repeat our parents' behaviors —
We repeat the emotional patterns beneath them.

So a parent who grew up with abandonment might over-attach.
A parent who was controlled might become overly permissive.
A parent who was criticized might avoid conflict entirely.

On the surface, these behaviors look different.
But underneath, they revolve around the same emotional wound.

And the child grows around that wound, shaping themselves to maintain connection.

Children don't complain —
they adjust.

The "Invisible Transfer" — Pain Without Words

Much of what parents pass down is not spoken.
It is felt in:
the tension in a room,

the heaviness after an argument,

the silence after disappointment,

the tiredness of a parent who is doing their best but running on empty.

A child's nervous system interprets these cues long before the mind can understand them.
Children absorb vibration, tone, tension, and unspoken emotion
the way a sponge absorbs water.
They don't need language to sense instability.
They feel it and normalize it —
because children always assume the environment is true.
If the home is anxious, anxiety becomes familiar.
If the home is emotionally cold, numbness becomes normal.
If the home is unpredictable, hypervigilance becomes instinct.
This shaping happens quietly —
the "invisible curriculum" of the home.

The Good News: Pain Is Not Permanent
Everything described above is real,
but it is also reversible.
Neuroscience shows that attachment patterns can be reshaped.
Epigenetic changes can soften.
Nervous systems can re-learn safety.
New emotional maps can be formed.
And one of the most hopeful findings in psychology is this:
Parents do not need to be healed to break the cycle.
They only need to be aware.
Awareness creates choice.
Choice creates new patterns.
New patterns create a different emotional climate.
When a parent slows down, breathes, listens, apologizes, repairs, reflects, or chooses
presence instead of repeating their past —
even once —
the cycle begins to shift.

Why This Matters for You

You did not become who you are by accident.
You learned to adapt to the garden you were planted in.
You grew in the direction that offered you the most safety.

But you are no longer the child shaping yourself around others.
You now have the power to turn toward the sun instead of the shadow.
You have the ability to raise your internal soil — to nourish, protect, and repair what was once missing.

You are not responsible for the pain you inherited.
You *are* responsible for how it lives in you now.

Not as punishment —
but as freedom. Healing your own wounds is how you end the inheritance.

5.3 — Becoming the Parent You Needed: Why Consciousness Changes Everything

There comes a moment in every adult life when you realize this simple, painful, liberating truth:

No one is coming to give you the childhood you deserved.
But you can create it now — from the inside out.

For many people, this realization arrives quietly. Not in a dramatic breakdown, but in small moments: when you're triggered by something minor, when you overreact and don't know why, when someone's tone feels like danger, when you suddenly feel five years old in an adult body.

This is the child within you speaking.

Not the imaginary "inner child" from clichés, but the very real bundle of neural pathways, emotional memories, and survival reflexes that formed before you had language, logic, or choice. The child who learned what love meant in the tone of your parents' voices, who learned what safety meant in the patterns of their nervous system, who learned who you were from the way they looked at you — or didn't.

And somewhere along the way, you became an adult who still carries that child's blueprint.

It's not your fault. It's simply how human development works.

But at a certain point, your life becomes an invitation: Will you continue living from the blueprint you inherited, or will you create a new one?

You Become the Parent Your Parents Couldn't Be

When we talk about "reparenting," it isn't about blaming your family. It's about recognizing that consciousness evolves. What your parents didn't heal, you now can.

Becoming a parent does not suddenly make someone wise, healed, or emotionally whole. It amplifies whatever is already inside us.

Children do not learn who they are through lectures or rules. They learn through absorption—through tone, presence, nervous-system signals, what is said and what is unsaid, how you treat yourself, how you treat others, and how you respond to life.

A child is not born into the world with emotional maps. They arrive like an untouched field—alive, open, ready to grow. The parents are the soil, the climate, the weather, the ecosystem the child grows inside.

This is why consciousness matters so deeply in parenting. Because no matter how much love a parent feels, unconscious pain leaks—through reactions, through stress, through emotional absence, through fear, through the stories a parent tells without words.

Why Consciousness Matters More Than Perfection

Consciousness is not about being calm all the time. It is not about speaking softly, parenting "correctly," or knowing the perfect psychological strategy.

Consciousness is the simple ability to notice yourself.

To notice when your voice becomes sharp. To notice when your chest tightens. To notice when you are reacting to your child, when really you are reacting to your own past. To notice when your anxiety, not the situation, is driving your words.

This noticing creates a sacred moment—a pause where the chain of generational pain can be stopped.

Without consciousness, parenting becomes reenactment.
With consciousness, parenting becomes transformation.

And if you are a parent already, this is not a sentence of guilt—it's a doorway into freedom. You don't have to be perfect. You only have to become aware.

Because *your child is not shaped by your flaws—they are shaped by your willingness to repair.*

The work is simple, but not easy: to sit with your triggers instead of projecting them, to feel your emotions instead of numbing them, to say "I'm sorry" when you lose your footing, to stay present when the old pattern wants to run the show.

Every time you pause, even for a breath, you interrupt a cycle that may have been running for generations.

This is how lineage changes: not through perfection, but through presence.

Children Inherit What Their Parents Cannot Face

A parent who never learned to feel their emotions will raise a child who cannot trust their own.

A parent who fears abandonment will teach, unconsciously, that love is something fragile.

A parent who carries unspoken grief will surround the child with emotional tension they cannot name.

A parent who never felt safe will struggle to offer safety.

Not because they don't want to—but because you cannot give what you have never learned to hold.

And yet none of this is destiny.

The moment a parent becomes aware of their own inherited wounds, something shifts: The cycle becomes visible, and visibility is the beginning of freedom.

Your children do not need a healed parent. They need a healing parent.

Your Child Is Your Mirror

Children reflect what parents cannot see in themselves.

They mirror your impatience. They mirror your tenderness. They mirror your fear of being judged. They mirror your longing to be loved gently.

This is not punishment. This is an opportunity.

Parenting can become one of the most powerful spiritual paths because it constantly invites you to grow where you once stopped growing. It exposes the wounds you hid.

It reveals the beliefs you forgot you carried. It asks: "Will you meet this moment with awareness or repetition?"

If You Don't Have Children, This Still Matters

Because there is a child inside you who has been waiting. Waiting for someone to listen. Waiting for someone to stay. Waiting for someone who will not abandon them when they cry, fear, reach out or fall apart.

You become that someone.

You become the stable adult presence your younger self never experienced. You become the voice of calm, the source of safety. You become the one who says:

"You are allowed to exist.

You are allowed to feel.

You are allowed to need."

This is not regression. This is integration.

You are repairing the foundation on which the rest of your life is built.

When you become the parent you needed, your capacity to love—yourself and others—expands naturally. You don't have to force self-worth or confidence or boundaries. They grow out of a healed internal relationship.

And if you ever choose to have children, or even if you never do, your presence in relationships—romantic, platonic, professional—becomes clearer, calmer, more compassionate.

Because when the inner child feels safe, the adult can finally live.

It Is Never Too Late to Break the Chain

Many people fear they have already "damaged" their children because they began healing later in life. But healing is not something you do alone—it is something your children experience with you.

Science shows that:

A parent who becomes more emotionally aware changes their child's attachment security

A parent who starts regulating their own nervous system helps the child's system reorganize

A parent who apologizes and repairs ruptures builds resilience in the child

A parent who learns to stay regulated during conflict teaches the child safety

You cannot go back and erase the past. But you can create a different future, one choice at a time.

Children adapt to you—and they will also adapt to your healing.

Every moment of awareness changes the emotional climate your child grows in.

Even if you already have children. Even if you did not begin perfectly. Even if you are learning late. Your awareness now reshapes everything.

Why Conscious Parents Raise Free Children

A conscious parent does not raise a perfect child. They raise a child who has permission to feel, to exist, to make mistakes, to be human.

A conscious parent teaches—not through words but through presence—that:

Emotions are safe

Connection is not conditional

Repair is possible

Boundaries are love

Authenticity is allowed

Fear can be felt without shame

Tenderness is strength

This is the gift of consciousness: your child becomes someone who does not need to spend adulthood repairing the damage of childhood.

They start life from safety, not survival. From wholeness, not fear.

Reparenting Is Not About Fixing the Past — It's About Changing the Future

You can't rewrite your childhood. But you can rewrite your patterns.

You can learn to speak to yourself with kindness instead of criticism. You can learn to regulate your nervous system before you react. You can learn to choose partners, friends, environments that nourish you. You can learn to stay present when your old self wants to run.

This is how wholeness grows.

Not from erasing your wounds—but from holding them with the love that was missing.

If you want your child to be confident, learn how to speak to yourself kindly.

If you want your child to feel safe, learn to regulate your own nervous system.

If you want your child to have boundaries, learn to hold your own.

If you want your child to feel loved, learn how to stay present with your own heart.

Your healing is not selfish. Your healing is the greatest gift you will ever give your child.

The Invitation

Reparenting is an ongoing relationship between who you were and who you are becoming.

Whether you have children now, hope to one day, or choose not to—consciousness is what breaks the cycle. Because without awareness, we pass down pain unconsciously. Not through words, but through nervous system patterns, emotional reflexes, and unhealed wounds.

Children don't inherit only your DNA—they inherit your state of being.

They absorb your tension, your avoidance, your anxiety, your loneliness, your grief. They also absorb your presence, your patience, your joy, your repair, your softness.

So if you are a parent now: it is never too late. You can repair it. You can pause. You can face your shadows so your child doesn't have to carry them. Even one conscious breath changes the future.

And if you will never have children: that inner child inside you is still yours to care for. Loving them is still sacred work. Healing them still transforms your world—and every relationship you will ever touch.

The cycle breaks the moment you say:

"I refuse to pass down what harmed me. This ends with me."

It's the moment you say to yourself:

"I'm here now.

I'm not leaving.

You're safe with me."

And from that moment forward, your entire life begins to shift.

Spiritual Meaning:

Parenting is not about shaping a child into who they should be; it is about becoming conscious enough that the child is free to become who they already are.

Quote:

"You are not too late. Every moment you choose awareness, your child inherits something new."

THE FAMILY BLUEPRINT: HOW WE INHERIT WOUNDS WE DON'T...

"Your healing becomes the home your children grow up inside."

Healing Practice:

Place your hand on your heart and breathe gently.
Say:

"I cannot change the past, but I can change the future.
The cycle ends with me."

"What part of my past is still speaking through me?"

Then choose one small moment today to respond with awareness instead of instinct.

"Your healing becomes the home your children grow up inside."

PART II - The Breaking Open

Pain after pain,

the cracks begin to open—

quiet at first,

then impossible to ignore.

Raw, tender,

I feel everything I tried to outrun

rising back to the surface.

Part of me wants to return

to who I was before,

to the familiar walls

that once protected me.

But I don't go back.

Something in me refuses.

Inside this opening,

I finally see myself—

the self beneath the fear,

the self I abandoned

just to survive.

The breaking is not destruction.

It is the moment

I come home to my own truth.

— author

Chapter 6
The Pattern Breaking Moment

There comes a moment in every person's life when the strategies that once kept them safe begin to feel too small. The identity that helped us navigate childhood, connection, love, and disappointment no longer fits as we grow. This moment rarely arrives during peace. It arrives when we meet someone who touches something old. It arrives in conflict. It arrives in silence. It arrives when we are confronted with the same emotional outcome we have lived through many times before.

It is not a loud moment.
It is usually quiet.
A sense of knowing rises inside the body before the mind has words for it.

For me, this realization came through relationships. I thought I was choosing new people, new dynamics, new stories. But I wasn't. I was choosing familiar emotional landscapes with different faces. I was responding not to the person in front of me, but to the memory behind me. I was reacting not from the present, but from the younger version of myself who had learned what love once required for survival.

This is not failure.
This is the nervous system trying to resolve something unfinished.

In psychology, this is known as repetition compulsion. The nervous system repeats familiar emotional situations not because it wants pain, but because it is trying to complete a story it did not have the capacity to understand when it first happened. It is the body's attempt to return to the moment where something split, overwhelmed, or silenced. The body keeps offering opportunities to repair what was never processed.

Spiritually, the same idea is expressed differently.

The lesson returns until it is integrated.

The pattern repeats until it is seen.

The wound continues to call for your attention until you stop abandoning it.

The universe does not punish.

It teaches through return.

We meet the same emotional dynamic in different relationships. Not because we are broken or unlucky, but because healing requires awareness, and awareness requires recognition. The same feeling shows up until we are ready to face it.

The Moment You Begin to Notice

The pattern-breaking moment is not dramatic.

It is subtle.

It sounds like:

"I've felt this before."

It feels like:

"I know this reaction. I know this tightening. I know this silence. I know this fear."

It is the quiet recognition that the intensity inside you does not match the moment outside you. The body responds with urgency, but the situation is small. The reaction is large because the memory is large.

This is the first doorway.

Awareness is the beginning of healing.

Not control.

Not change.

Just awareness.

You cannot transform what you cannot see.

Just as a doctor cannot treat a wound that has not been diagnosed, you cannot change a pattern that has not yet been recognized. Without awareness, we continue to leave situations while bringing the same survival pattern with us. The story changes locations, but the author has not awakened.

The pattern does not end when the relationship ends.
The pattern ends when consciousness enters.

Seeing the Pattern with Compassion

This is where *The Power of Now* by Eckhart Tolle becomes deeply relevant. Tolle explains that suffering continues only when we remain unconscious of the process unfolding inside us. The moment we observe ourselves, even if only for a few seconds, the pattern begins to loosen.

Awareness creates distance.
Distance creates space.
Space interrupts automatic reaction.

In that space, something new becomes possible.
You may not change the reaction immediately.
You may still feel the rush of fear or the urge to pull away or cling.
You may still feel the heat of anger or the collapse of withdrawal.

But now you are aware that it is happening.
This awareness is not small.
This awareness is the shift.

The moment you say inside yourself,
"This is the old pattern,"
you are no longer inside the reaction.
You are witnessing it.

Witnessing is awakening.

The Ego's Role in Keeping the Pattern Alive

To soften a pattern, there must also be surrender.
Not surrender in the sense of giving up or suppressing yourself.
Surrender in the sense of loosening the grip of the identity you built to survive.

People misunderstand ego.
The ego is not arrogance or selfishness.
The ego is the protective identity formed in childhood to keep us safe.

The ego is the voice that says:

"I know who I am."
"I know how to protect myself."
"I cannot change this."
"I must control the situation."
"If I let go, I will get hurt again."

The ego does not trust the unknown.
The ego trusts familiarity.

Even if familiarity was painful.

In *Ego is the Enemy*, Ryan Holiday describes how the ego would rather repeat known suffering than risk unfamiliar peace. The ego is not logical. It is protective. The ego is the child inside us who learned that survival required being guarded, alert, reactive, pleasing, silent, angry, or strong.

The ego is not the enemy.
The ego is the child's shield.

Surrender is not destroying the ego.
Surrender is speaking gently to the part of yourself that learned to guard so fiercely.

Surrender is saying:

"You protected me when I did not know how to protect myself.
I see you.
I thank you.
But we are not in that environment anymore."

Surrender is choosing freedom over familiarity.

The Day I Realized the Pattern Was Mine

The moment my pattern began to break was not when I was in emotional collapse. It was not during a heartbreak. It was not in pain. It was in a simple conversation where the emotional intensity I felt did not match what was happening.

Something in me recognized:
"This reaction is older than this moment."

That realization softened me.

The person in front of me was not the threat.
The threat lived in memory.
The emotion belonged to a younger version of me.

This was the moment the child inside me came into view.

Healing begins not when we fix the reaction.
Healing begins when we ask:
"What part of me is trying to be protected right now?"
The question turns the reaction from panic into tenderness.
The reaction is not a failure.
The reaction is a message.

The Heart Does Not Heal Through Force
You cannot break a pattern by overpowering it.
You cannot force yourself into secure love.
You cannot silence fear with logic.
You cannot shame yourself into emotional maturity.
Healing does not come from control.
Healing comes from gentleness.
The pattern is not the enemy.
The ego is not the enemy.
They are both expressions of the self trying to protect the heart.
The only question now is:
Are the old strategies still needed?
You learned to protect yourself before you had words, choices, or power.
Now you do.
The pattern was created in a moment when you could not choose.
But you are not that child anymore.
You have awareness now.
You have support now.
You have breath now.
You have time now.
You have capacity now.
The pattern is not broken through force.
The pattern dissolves through recognition.
Awareness opens the door.
Presence keeps it open.
Compassion invites the child inside you to step forward.
This is the work.

Spiritual Meaning:

The moment you recognize the pattern is the moment your inner self returns to the surface. It is not a transformation in the future. It is remembrance in the present.

Quote:

"You cannot change what you have not yet seen, and the moment you see the pattern, healing has already begun."

Healing Practice:

Write this sentence and complete it without judgment:

"The part of me who reacts this way is trying to protect…"

Let the words come.

Do not correct.

Do not analyze.

Just witness.

Chapter 7
The Body Speaks What the Mind Cannot

There are some truths the mind is not yet ready to speak,
but the body speaks to them anyway.

Not with words, but with sensation.

A tightening in the chest.

A heaviness in the limbs.

A sudden numbness.

A rising heat.

A flutter of panic.

A shutting down.

These reactions often appear at the *exact* moments we wish to be most present — in love, in closeness, in vulnerability, in honesty.

We try to reason with ourselves:

"Why am I reacting like this?"

"Nothing is actually happening."

"Why can't I just relax?"

"Why do I shut down when I want to open?"

But the reaction happens before thought.
This is because the body remembers what the mind has tried to forget.

Memory Stored as Sensation

Not all memories have words.
Not all pain becomes story.
Some experiences enter before we had language.
Before we could say:
"This hurt me."
"This scared me."
"This was too much."
So the body stored the memory for us.
This is called implicit memory.
It lives not in the mind, but in the muscles, the breath, the heartbeat, the nervous system.
The body remembers:
The tone of a voice raised in anger.
The silence of emotional distance.
The feeling of being ignored, unseen, or too much.
The anticipation of conflict.
The shame of not being enough.
The confusion of love that was warm one day and distant the next.
The body remembers the atmosphere —
even when the mind has forgotten the details.

The Nervous System Protects Before We Understand

The body has one primary question:
"Am I safe?"
This question is answered through sensation, not thoughts.
Before the mind forms meaning, the nervous system interprets emotional atmosphere through a process called neuroception.
This happens faster than conscious awareness — in less than a second.
Which means:
Your body can be triggered
even if your mind believes everything is fine.

This is not overreaction.
This is protection.
Your nervous system is not reacting to *the present*.
It is reacting to the past trying to repeat.

When the Body Reacts, It Is Completing an Old Story

Peter Levine, in *Waking the Tiger*, explains:

"Trauma is not what happened.
Trauma is what remains in the body when there was no one there to help you process what happened."

When we felt overwhelmed as children — emotionally or physically —
our body began a stress response
(breath held, muscles contracted, energy rising)
but we were too young to complete it.

So the stress response froze in the body.
The nervous system said:

"Later.
We will finish this later.
When it is safe."

And "later" became adulthood.

This is why small things can feel big now.

Not because they are big —
but because they touch what was never finished.

The Four Common Body Responses to Emotional Overwhelm

1. Tight Chest / Holding Breath

Protection of vulnerability.
The body shields the heart when it remembers emotional danger.

2. Heat Rising / Anger / Pressure

The sympathetic nervous system preparing to defend, speak, or escape.

3. Numbness / Blankness

The freeze response.
The body reduces sensation to prevent overwhelm.

4. Shaking / Restlessness
The nervous system trying to discharge emotional energy that was never expressed.
None of these reactions are signs of weakness.
They are signs the body is trying to protect you.
The body is not sabotaging you —
it is trying to finish what it could not finish when you were young.

Understanding the Body's Language
The body never reacts without reason.
The body is always communicating:

Tightness → "Something feels emotionally risky."

Numbness → "This feeling was once too much to bear."

Heat → "I needed to defend myself once."

Shaking → "I am trying to release what I held back."

The question is not:
"How do I stop this?"
The question is:
"What is this sensation protecting?"
The body is the storyteller
of the parts of us that have not yet been spoken.

Interoception: The Art of Listening to the Body
Interoception is the ability to feel the inside of your body.
Most of us learned to disconnect from this early.
We were taught to think, not to sense.
To appear "fine," even when the body was distressed.
Healing requires returning to inner awareness:
Feeling breath moving in the chest

Feeling the weight of the body on the ground

Feeling warmth in the hands

Feeling the rise and fall of the belly

Not judging it.
Not fixing it.
Just *noticing*.
   This is how the body begins to trust again.
   Presence is the medicine.

Somatic Healing: Completing the Unfinished Story
   The body needs to complete what was once interrupted.
   This does not happen through analyzing or talking.
It happens through gentle, slow, safe sensation awareness.
   Pendulation (Peter Levine)
   Move your awareness between a place of tension and a place of comfort.
Back and forth. Slowly.
This teaches the nervous system that it is safe to feel without being overwhelmed.

   Titration
   Healing happens in small doses.
You do not dive into the deepest part of the wound.
You enter slowly, breath by breath.
   Grounding Touch
   Place one hand on your chest and one hand on your lower belly.
Feel the warmth of your own presence.
The body responds to touch that communicates,
"I am here now."
   Breath as Permission
   Instead of trying to control the breath,
let the breath soften into the body.
   Inhale gently through the nose.
Exhale slowly, like sighing into rest.

This tells the nervous system:
We are not in danger anymore.

Spiritual Meaning:

The body does not interrupt your life;
it leads you back to the parts of yourself that still need love.

Quote:

"My body is not betraying me; it is remembering for me."

Healing Practice:

The next time your body reacts, do not try to change it.
Place your hand on the sensation and whisper internally:

"I hear you.
I am here now.
You are safe to feel."

Repeat three breaths.
Let the emotion move in its own time.

Chapter 8
Meeting the Shadow Self

There comes a moment in every healing journey when the light we have gathered invites us to look into the dark.

Not to suffer.

Not to break.

But to understand.

The shadow is not the enemy.

The shadow is the part of us that was left alone for too long.

It is the unheard anger.

The unspoken grief.

The child who never had space to feel.

The self who learned to hide to survive.

Most of us spend years avoiding this part of ourselves because we believe it is dangerous.

But the shadow is not danger.

The shadow is emotion that was never allowed to be seen.

When you meet your shadow, you are not meeting something broken.

You are meeting the part of you that tried the hardest to stay alive.

What is the Shadow?

MEETING THE SHADOW SELF

In psychology, Carl Jung used the word shadow to describe the parts of ourselves we learned to hide:

The feelings that were labeled as too much.

The needs that were ignored.

The anger we were punished for.

The sensitivity we were told to toughen.

The dreams that were laughed at.

The fear that was never comforted.

These parts of us did not disappear.

They went inward.

They became:

The tension in the jaw

The racing thoughts before sleep

The panic before intimacy

The irritation that rises too fast

The numbness that appears when things get close

The exhaustion that does not match the day

The shadow is the emotional self we abandoned in order to survive.

Not because we were weak.

But because we were *children*, and children adapt to stay safe.

Spiritually, the Shadow is Not Darkness

Spiritual teachings often describe the shadow as the unloved self.

The part of you that still waits to be welcomed home.

It is not an enemy to conquer.

It is not a flaw to fix.

It is not a wound to perform healing on.

The shadow is a door.

On the other side of that door is your softness, your truth, your aliveness.

To meet the shadow is to return to yourself.

Why the Shadow Appears Most in Relationships

The shadow does not appear when life is easy.

It appears when life becomes intimate.

Because intimacy is where we are asked to be seen.

The shadow emerges when someone gets close enough to touch something unfinished.

This is why:

You may feel rage at small things

You may withdraw when someone loves you

You may chase love that does not choose you

You may feel numb when you want to feel close

You may get defensive when someone tries to understand you

These are not character flaws.

These are protective responses that developed when you were too young to explain your pain.

The shadow appears not to ruin love but to protect you from love that feels unsafe.

It is the child inside you saying:

"I remember what closeness cost.

Please do not let it happen again."

The Shadow is the Young Self Frozen in Time

Every painful emotional memory stores a younger self inside you.

A self who did not get to finish their story.

A child who needed:

Comfort but got silence

Safety but got instability

Love but got conditions

Presence but got withdrawal

Space to feel but got rushed maturity

This child still lives inside the body.

When something touches the old wound, the child reacts first.

Not the adult.

This is why sometimes you look back and think:

"That reaction wasn't me."

"It felt like someone younger was in control."

"Why did I shut down so fast?"

"Why did I get so angry over something small?"

Because it wasn't you now.

It was you then.

And that part of you has never been met.

Meeting the Shadow is a Reunion, Not a Battle

Many people approach shadow work like a challenge:
"Let me dig deep."
"Let me break myself open."
"Let me force healing now."
This is not medicine.
This is reenactment of survival.
The shadow does not open under force.
The shadow opens under warmth.
Meeting the shadow gently sounds like:
"I see you."
"You didn't deserve what happened."
"You were doing the best you could."
"I won't leave you now."
"You do not have to protect me anymore."
Healing is not dramatic.
Healing is a quiet, slow, steady presence.

How to Recognize the Shadow in Daily Life

The shadow speaks in the moments when your reaction feels louder than the situation.
For example:
Someone says, "I need space,"
and your body feels abandoned.
Someone says, "I love you,"
and your chest tightens.
Someone asks, "What's wrong,"
and you cannot find your voice.
Someone apologizes,
and you still feel unsafe.
Someone tries to understand you,
and you get defensive.
These reactions are signals, not failures.
They say:
"There is something here that has not yet been held."

How to Approach the Shadow Safely

We do not dive into pain.

We sit beside it.
Slow down the moment of reaction
Place one hand on your chest.
Feel the body, not the story.
Name the part that is speaking
Say silently:
"A younger part of me is here."
Let the child speak
Not through sentences.
Through sensation.
Offer presence, not fixing
You do not need to understand everything yet.
You only need to stay.
The shadow heals through being accompanied.

A Spiritual Truth
You do not need to become someone new.
You need to return to the one who has been waiting inside you.
The shadow is not darkness.
The shadow is unmet light.
When you turn toward it, gently, you begin to see:
There was nothing wrong with you.
You were overwhelmed.
You were alone with too much.
You survived the only way you could.
And now you have the capacity to return.

Spiritual Meaning:
The shadow is not the place you are meant to fear.
It is the doorway to the part of you that has always known love.
Quote:
"The part of me I ran from is the part of me that needed my arms the most."
Healing Practice:
Sit somewhere quiet.

MEETING THE SHADOW SELF

Place your hand on your heart.
Close your eyes.
Ask gently inside:
"Little one, what are you still afraid of?"
Do not rush the answer.
Let the child speak in sensation.
Stay. Stay. Stay

Chapter 9
The Soul's View of Suffering

There are seasons in life when pain becomes impossible to outrun.

The strategies that once protected us stop working. The noise gets too loud.

The distractions lose their effect. The laughter no longer hides anything.

The heart begins to speak, not softly, but with a steady, unignorable pulse.

This moment is not a collapse.

It is a calling.

A calling to come back to yourself.

Most of us do not arrive here willingly.

We arrive because the world outside us can no longer keep us from the world within us.

We arrive when the cost of avoidance becomes heavier than the cost of truth.

I once believed that if I turned inward, there would be only darkness.

I feared that if I looked closely at my pain, I would drown inside it.

So I kept myself moving — fast, bright, loud, busy.

I laughed instead of cried.

I entertained instead of revealed.

I survived instead of lived.

But pain is patient.

> *It waits.*
>
> *Not to punish you,*
>
> *but because it is yours.*
>
> *-Author*

The Fear of Entering the Inner World

Many people fear their inner world for the same reason I once did:
   We are afraid that if we enter the darkness inside us,
   we will not find our way out.
   But darkness is not the absence of light.
   It is the space where light has not yet been met.
   The wound does not want to consume you.
   It wants to *be witnessed*.
   Suffering is the body and soul asking to be seen.
   When the pain is ignored, minimized, or outrun, it grows louder.
   When it is met with presence, it softens.
   The soul does not see suffering as punishment.
   The soul sees suffering as unfinished love.
   Love that was never given.
   Love that was never received.
   Love that froze in time waiting for you to come back for it.
   The Spiritual Nature of Suffering
   Buddha did not say life is suffering.
   He said suffering comes from resisting reality.
   Pain is part of life: love, loss, longing, attachment, memory.
   Suffering is what happens when we refuse to feel that pain.
   I resisted for years because I thought feeling pain would destroy me.
   Instead, avoiding pain was what kept me separated from myself.
   Suffering asks one simple question:
   Can you stay?
   Can you stay with yourself while the heart trembles?
   Can you stay with your breath when the past rises?

Can you stay without abandoning yourself?

Not analyzing.

Not fixing.

Not escaping.

Just staying.

This is where transformation begins.

The Science Behind the Soul

Psychology names what the soul already knows.

When emotional experiences overwhelm a child, the nervous system stores the memory in the body.

Not as a story — but as sensation, tension, breath, silence.

This is why meditation can feel terrifying at first.

Meditation is not relaxation.

Meditation is meeting yourself.

When we sit still and close our eyes, the mind stops running long enough for the body to speak.

The body says:

Here is the sadness you never cried.

Here is the fear you swallowed.

Here is the love you didn't receive.

Here is the longing you learned to hide.

This is not regression.

This is remembrance.

Neuroscience confirms this.

During meditation, the default mode network — the part of the brain that maintains identity and self-story — begins to quiet.

When this happens, suppressed emotional memory surfaces.

Not to overwhelm you.

To be released.

The body does not reveal anything you are not ready to meet.

The Moment Everything Turns

Healing does not begin with strength.

Healing begins with honesty.

The moment I whispered to myself,

with no performance,

no shield,

no cleverness:

"I am hurting."

Everything shifted.

Not all at once.

Not dramatically.

Just enough to breathe differently.

The heart softens by a millimeter at a time.

The inner door opens the width of a fingertip.

That's enough.

When the Universe Teaches Through Repetition

Life repeats lessons.

Not because we are slow.

But because the lesson is holy.

We meet the same type of partner, the same argument, the same emotional pain — in different bodies, different rooms, different seasons.

This is not coincidence.

This is the universe saying:

"This is the place that needs your love."

Suffering is where the soul is asking to awaken.

The universe is not cruel.

The universe is persistent.

The Shadow Is Not the Enemy

The shadow is simply the part of you that learned to protect you.

The shadow is:

The part that braced when things got close.

The part that learned to smile when you wanted to scream.

The part that walked alone because no one came.

The part that stayed strong when you were breaking.

Your shadow is not trying to harm you.

Your shadow has been trying to save you.

But now, you do not need saving.

You need belonging — with yourself.

THE SOUL'S VIEW OF SUFFERING

How Meditation Opens the Inner World

Meditation is not about clearing the mind.

It is about clearing space for truth.

The breath becomes the doorway.

The breath is the rope you hold while descending into the inner dark.

When you breathe slowly:

The vagus nerve signals safety.

The amygdala softens.

The body loosens its grip.

The mind stops fighting.

The doorway opens.

And inside, there is not a void.

There is a small, steady light.

A spark.

The same spark you came into the world with.

The same spark that has survived every version of you.

This spark does not need to be found.

It needs to be *remembered*.

Your Story Becomes Medicine

You did not learn this from books.

You learned this from living.

You learned it from nights you held yourself alone.

From mornings you rose without knowing how.

From days you walked with grief in your lungs and kept going.

From heartbreak that cracked you open in places you didn't know existed.

Your suffering gave you depth.

Your depth gives you compassion.

Your compassion makes you capable of loving in ways that are rare in this world.

Your story is not something to hide.

Your story is medicine.

For yourself first.

Then, slowly, for others.

This Is the Soul's View:

You were never broken.

You were becoming.
You were never lost.
You were searching.
You were never weak.
You were protecting something tender inside you.
You were not late.
You were ripening.

Spiritual Meaning:
Suffering is where the heart returns to itself.
Not through force.
Through remembering.

Quote:
"The pain I feared was the doorway back to myself."

Healing Practice:
Sit with your breath for 2 minutes.
Not to change anything.
Not to fix anything.
Just to be with yourself.
Whisper softly:
"I am learning to stay."
"I am safe to feel."
"I am coming home to myself."

THE SOUL'S VIEW OF SUFFERING

PART III The Returning

There comes a moment

when the heaviness loosens—

not all at once,

but gently,

like light slipping back

through a window

I forgot was there.

I feel myself returning, slowly, honestly,

as if my spirit

is walking home

after years of being lost

in its own shadows.

The fear is softer now. The world feels wider.

And somewhere inside, a small, steady truth rises:

I am allowed to begin again.

Not as who I was,

but as who I'm becoming— stronger, clearer, finally breathing

without shrinking.

This return

is not a step backward.

It is the first step

toward myself.

— author

Chapter 10
Safety in the Body

The moment you stop running from yourself, silence begins to hum beneath the noise.

Your pulse softens. The world sharpens. You realize the earth has been holding you the entire time.

Safety is not the absence of threat; it is the remembrance of belonging.

It lives in the way your breath moves when you finally let it.

It lives in the ground that never left.

It lives inside your skin, waiting for you to come home.

— *Author*

Scientific Grounding: The Biology of Safety

Before healing can take root, the body must believe the danger is over. You can think positive thoughts, repeat affirmations, or write pages in a journal, but if the nervous system has not received the message of safety, the body continues to operate as if survival is still required. The muscles hold tension as memory; the diaphragm contracts to guard the heart; the breath shortens to stay ready.

Neuroscience explains that the human nervous system has three main states: fight-or-flight, freeze, and rest-and-connect. Dr Stephen Porges, in his *Polyvagal Theory*, describes how the vagus nerve—stretching from brain stem to heart, lungs, and gut—regulates these states. When the vagus nerve signals safety, heart rate variability increases, digestion resumes, and the voice naturally softens. When it signals threat, the body braces, blood flow shifts to the limbs, and perception narrows. Healing therefore begins not in the intellect but in the vagus nerve's language of rhythm and tone.

Every inhale activates the sympathetic branch, preparing the body to engage; every exhale activates the parasympathetic branch, restoring calm. That is why slow, lengthened exhalations are an ancient yet scientifically proven way to re-educate the body toward peace. Neuroscientist Andrew Huberman notes that consistent daily breathing—especially the "physiological sigh," two short inhales followed by a long exhale—lowers cortisol, slows the heartbeat, and communicates to the brain that life is no longer an emergency.

Safety is thus learned through repetition, not reasoning. Each time you exhale fully, you are teaching your cells that they can stand down. Each time you stretch, yawn, or unclench the jaw, you send data upward to the brain saying, "We are safe enough now to rest." Over weeks, these micro-messages accumulate until calm becomes a baseline rather than a rare event.

The body's story of safety is written in sensation. It is not forced. It is practiced—through gentle breathwork, mindful movement, and the willingness to feel the small shifts that mark recovery.

Spiritual Integration: The Ancient Language of the Body

Long before neuroscience, wisdom traditions understood this. Yogic texts described *prana*, the life-breath that balances body and spirit. Buddhist monks spoke of *anapanasati*, awareness of breathing as the gateway to liberation. Sufi mystics swirled until the heart outpaced the mind, using rhythm to merge with presence. Indigenous healers placed bare feet on the earth to exchange currents with the living ground. Though their words differ, they all point to one truth: stillness enters only where the body feels safe to open.

Modern culture often separates spirituality from physiology, yet they are the same conversation spoken in two dialects. Science measures the heartbeat; spirituality listens to it. Science names oxytocin, dopamine, and serotonin; spirituality calls them trust, joy, and peace. When you combine the two, healing becomes both measurable and mysterious—a dialogue between neuron and soul.

When you settle your breath, you are not performing a ritual from the past; you are continuing humanity's oldest prayer: *I am still here.*

Personal Reflection and Reader Practice

The first time I truly felt safe in my own body was not during meditation or therapy—it was on an ordinary morning when the noise in my head went quiet. There was no great insight, only the steady rhythm of breath and a sense of space inside my ribs. For the first time, I could hear the hum of the refrigerator, the birds outside, my own heartbeat, and none of it felt like background chaos. It felt like belonging. The calm did not come from thinking positively; it came from allowing the body to exist without demand.

Readers often expect safety to arrive as permanent peace, but it begins as a flicker—a single exhale that doesn't feel forced. You might experience it after a long cry, during slow movement, or in the stillness that follows honest conversation. That is the body's way of saying, *I can stop running for a moment.*

To cultivate this, start where you are. Sit or stand in a way that feels grounded. Notice your feet touching the floor or the weight of your body on a chair. Take one full breath in through your nose. Let it fill the belly first, then the ribs, then the chest. Hold for a gentle heartbeat. Exhale through the mouth as if you are fogging a window. Do this three times. Nothing mystical—just biology meeting awareness. Over time, this practice teaches your nervous system that presence is not a threat. Huberman's research supports this: repeated somatic calm rewires the neural pathways of vigilance into pathways of trust. The brain learns that stillness is survivable.

When the world feels loud again, return to the body as to an anchor. You do not have to fix anything—only witness. If your chest tightens, place a hand there and whisper, "I hear you." If tears arrive, let them. They are proof the body is thawing. This is how trauma leaves: not in one revelation but through a thousand tiny permissions to feel.

Spiritual Integration and Broader Meaning

Ancient teachers described this same process through symbols. The Taoists called it *wu wei*—effortless action. The Buddhists called it right mindfulness. Christian mystics called it resting in grace. All point toward the same truth: the more gently you inhabit yourself, the more life flows through you. Safety is not earned through control; it is invited through trust. When the breath becomes steady, the spirit begins to listen. In that stillness, intuition—what many traditions name the voice of the soul—rises quietly from within the chest.

Science calls this interoception: the brain's ability to sense internal states. Spirituality calls it presence. Both describe the same phenomenon—the moment you notice your body as part of the living world, not separate from it. Trees breathe carbon dioxide; you breathe oxygen; the exchange never stops. The pulse in your wrist beats to the same rhythm that moves the tides. Safety, then, is not isolation; it is reconnection.

Closing Reflection

Safety is learned the way music is learned—through repetition until rhythm replaces effort. Every slow breath, every kind self-touch, every pause before reacting is a note in the body's new song. One day you wake and realize that your breath is long again, your shoulders hang easily, and the world feels wider. That is the body remembering freedom.

We are not repairing a broken machine; we are re-entering a home that waited patiently with the lights on. Healing does not mean the storms end; it means you know how to return to shelter. The body was never against you—it was guarding the door until you came back.

Spiritual Meaning:
Your body is not the enemy of your healing; it is the doorway into it.

Quote:
"Safety is not something you find. It is something you learn to feel again."

Healing Practice:
Sit quietly, place one hand on your heart and one on your belly. Inhale through the

nose for four counts, exhale through the mouth for six. Whisper, "I am here." Repeat until the mind listens. Do this daily, not to chase calm but to remind the body that it already knows the way home.

Chapter 11
Speaking to Inner Child

Somewhere within you, a small voice waits beneath the noise.
It hides behind your practiced smile, behind the way you say "I'm fine."
It has watched you grow taller, move faster, love harder, yet it still curls its knees against the same quiet ache.
That voice does not belong to memory; it belongs to presence.
It is the child who never stopped hoping someone would finally listen.

— *Author*

Scientific & Psychological Grounding

Modern psychology agrees with ancient wisdom: every adult carries earlier developmental selves inside the nervous system. John Bradshaw, whose work *Home Coming* helped define "inner-child" theory, explained that this part of the psyche is not metaphor but biology—an imprint of neural pathways formed before language. During infancy and early childhood, the brain operates primarily in right-hemisphere emotional processing. Experiences of tone, gaze, touch, and rhythm shape the amygdala and limbic circuits that later govern attachment and trust.

Alice Miller called the child "the prisoner of the past who still waits for empathy." When early environments provide inconsistent care, the child adapts by reading danger before it appears. These adaptations—hyper-alertness, people-pleasing, perfectionism, withdrawal—become coded into the autonomic nervous system as survival responses. They remain active long after the external threat is gone.

Neuroscientist Allan Schore's research on affect regulation shows that repeated attunement—being soothed when distressed—literally wires the brain for self-soothing in adulthood. Conversely, repeated neglect or emotional unpredictability wires it for hyper-vigilance. This is why a calm conversation can suddenly feel unsafe, why praise can trigger discomfort, why love can ignite fear. The body is not confused; it is remembering.

Dr Gabor Maté expands on this in *When the Body Says No*: emotions suppressed in childhood re-emerge through the body's physiology. Stress hormones, immune responses, and chronic tension all speak the language of unmet need. The adult who collapses into exhaustion after care-taking everyone else is reliving the child who earned love through service. The adult who shuts down during conflict is echoing the child who survived by disappearing. These are not flaws in character; they are extensions of earlier intelligence.

The Biology of Re-Parenting

Healing requires new experiences of safety recorded through the vagus nerve and prefrontal cortex. Each time you respond to discomfort with curiosity instead of judgment, you are re-educating your nervous system. Psychologist Richard Schwartz's Internal Family Systems model describes this as leading from "Self"—the compassionate adult consciousness capable of caring for inner parts. When you breathe slowly, speak gently inside your mind, or visualize holding your younger self, you activate parasympathetic pathways that calm limbic alarm. Over months, those repeated states become traits.

This is why meditation and somatic awareness are effective forms of re-parenting: they give the inner child a different ending to the same story. Instead of being ignored, the feeling is witnessed. Instead of being silenced, it is heard. Neuroplasticity allows the brain to update its prediction that emotion equals danger. The body begins to learn that love can coexist with safety.

Spiritual & Philosophical Integration

Every spiritual tradition carries a story about returning to innocence. In Christianity, it is "becoming as little children" to enter the kingdom of heaven. In Buddhism, it is *beginner's mind*—seeing the world without preconception. In Sufism, it is polishing the mirror of the heart until it reflects only light. Psychologically, these parables point to the same process: healing the child within is the act of clearing the layers of defence that formed around purity.

Carl Jung called this return "the integration of the child-archetype," the meeting of the conscious adult with the instinctive, feeling self. He wrote that the child symbolises potential—what we lost when we traded wonder for certainty. When you close your eyes and greet that small presence, you are not indulging nostalgia; you are re-connecting neural and spiritual circuits that were severed by fear.

Mindfulness teacher Thích Nhất Hạnh offered a simple way to do this. He would place his hand on his heart and say, "Dear little one, I am here for you." Nothing elaborate, no psychological jargon—just presence. Presence is what the inner child always needed and rarely received. When you offer it now, you collapse the distance between who you were and who you are.

Personal Reflection & Reader Dialogue Practice

There was a time I believed strength meant ignoring pain. I kept moving forward, collecting achievements, pretending that progress meant peace. Then one day, during quiet meditation, I felt a tug in my chest—small, hesitant, familiar. It was as if someone had been knocking softly for years. When I listened, I heard words I hadn't expected: *"You left me behind."*

That voice was not a memory; it was alive. I realised my adult life was built around protecting a child who still felt unsafe. My perfectionism, my humour, even my independence were strategies to keep her from feeling small again. The moment I turned toward her, everything began to make sense.

You can do the same. Find a quiet space. Breathe slowly until the body settles. Imagine the younger you—perhaps age five, seven, or twelve—standing a few steps away. Notice their expression, posture, the way they hold their shoulders. Ask gently, *"What do you want to tell me?"* Do not fill the silence. Wait. Sometimes the child will whisper a single word—*tired, lonely, scared*. Sometimes they will show you images instead of sentences. Trust whatever comes. The language of the inner world is symbolic, not logical.

When answers arrive, resist the urge to interpret or fix. Simply say, "I hear you." Then ask, "What do you need from me now?" The reply might surprise you: *Play with me. Stop working so much. Let me rest. Stop pretending.* Each request is an invitation to live differently. Each act of kindness toward yourself rewrites the emotional blueprint that once equated love with effort.

You may notice tears, warmth, or a trembling sensation. These are signs that neural pathways long frozen are thawing. Dr Peter Levine calls this "completing the interrupted response." Emotion finally moves through the body the way it wanted to decades ago. Stay with it. Breathe through it. When the wave passes, you will feel a quiet spaciousness where tension once lived. That space is your nervous system expanding to include the child instead of suppressing them.

Integrating the Two Selves

Over time, the dialogue between adult and child becomes second nature. When you feel anxious before a meeting, you recognise whose fear it is. When you over-apologise, you notice which part of you still believes safety depends on being pleasing. This awareness transforms reaction into relationship. You become both parent and child, protector and protected.

To nurture this connection, create small rituals of care. Some people write letters to their younger selves; others keep a childhood photo nearby as a reminder of tenderness. Speak aloud phrases like, "You're doing great," or "It's safe to rest." It may feel strange at first, but repetition teaches the brain that compassion is allowed. Safety, again, is learned through experience.

When frustration arises and you snap at yourself, pause. Instead of judgment, ask, "Would I speak to a five-year-old this way?" The tone softens instantly. This is how re-parenting becomes muscle memory: not through grand insights but through daily micro-moments of gentleness.

Closing Reflection

The child inside you is not fragile; they are sacred. They carried you through chaos without the tools you now have. They deserve reverence, not repair. Each time you listen instead of suppress, you rewrite the story of what love feels like. Eventually ,the boundary between "inner child" and "adult self" dissolves, and there is only one being—whole, mature, tender, free.

Spiritual Meaning:

To speak to the inner child is to return to the original self waiting to be loved back into wholeness.

Quote:

"You were not weak. You were surviving. Now you are safe to be soft."

Healing Practice:

Sit quietly. Place one hand on your heart and the other on your belly. Breathe slowly. Visualise the younger you sitting beside you. Whisper:

"I am here now. I won't leave you."

Stay for five slow breaths. Let them feel you.

Chapter 12
Healing Intimacy

Intimacy is not something we learn as adults.

It is something we remember in our bones.

It begins in the first moments of life — in how we were held, how we were seen,

how the air around us felt when we cried.

If the voice that soothed was steady, the body learned to open.

If the voice was sharp, distant, or absent, the body learned to guard.

Long before we spoke words like love or touch,

we learned what safety felt like — and whether it could be trusted.

That first lesson never left us.

It echoes quietly beneath every embrace,

every silence, every moment we reach for closeness and then hesitate.

— Author

12.1— How Trauma Shapes Intimacy & Desire

The Neurobiology of Trauma and Intimacy

The body is a sacred memory.

Every breath, every pulse, every instinct carries the story of how we learned to survive.

When safety was uncertain, the nervous system became a guardian.

It began to scan constantly — for tone, for tension, for danger hiding behind a smile.

Dr. Stephen Porges calls this *neuroception* — the body's way of sensing safety or threat before the mind can think.

If early love felt unpredictable, the body learned to expect both warmth and pain.

The heart, which once opened easily, began to calculate risk.

The breath shortened. The muscles braced. The soul stayed half-ready to run.

Trauma is not just a wound of the mind — it is a reorganization of how the body reads reality.

The autonomic system — the same one that keeps the heart beating and lungs moving — begins to misinterpret tenderness as danger.

Even gentle touch can awaken alarm. Even kindness can feel suspicious.

This is why some people crave love but feel panic when it arrives.

The paradox is not weakness; it is intelligence.

The body is saying, "I remember when this feeling meant I might be hurt."

And yet, beneath the vigilance, another voice whispers:

I still want to trust again.

That voice is your soul reminding you that the body was not meant to live only in defence —

it was meant to feel the sacred rhythm of connection.

Attachment and Relational Patterns

Attachment is the earliest mirror of love.

As children, we learn whether our emotions are welcomed or inconvenient.

We learn whether love stays or disappears when we need it most.

Dr. Judith Herman writes that trauma "organizes life around the search for safety."

Every adult relationship becomes a reflection of this search —

sometimes calm, sometimes chaotic, often confusing.
When love was consistent, the body learned that closeness could be trusted.
When love was conditional, it learned that safety must be earned.
When love was frightening, it learned to seek distance even while longing for warmth.
These patterns do not come from logic; they come from the nervous system.
They are written into our breath and posture, our tone and timing, our unspoken fears of being too much or not enough.
The anxious lover leans forward — needing reassurance that love will not disappear.
The avoidant lover steps back — needing space to breathe without being swallowed.
The disorganized lover does both — reaching and retreating, aching and afraid.
None of these patterns mean you are broken.
They mean you adapted to an emotional climate that asked you to protect yourself.
Spiritually, attachment is the way the soul learns about *trust*.
It is how we practice being held — not just by people, but by life itself.
Every heartbreak, every withdrawal, every reunion is part of the curriculum of returning home to safety within.

The Body's Logic of Repetition

The universe speaks through repetition.
What we have not yet understood, we meet again —
not to punish, but to complete.
When the same emotional theme reappears in different faces,
It is life showing us the pattern that longs for healing.
You may find yourself drawn to the same kind of partner,
having the same arguments,
feeling the same ache,
even after you promised, "never again."
This is not failure.
This is the soul's intelligence repeating the lesson until it becomes wisdom.
Psychology calls this *repetition compulsion* —
the unconscious pull to recreate what once hurt,
hoping this time we can rewrite the ending.
Spiritually, it is the law of resonance:
we attract the frequency we most need to transform.
When you find yourself inside a familiar emotional storm, pause and ask:

"What is this experience trying to reveal?"
Not "Why is this happening to me," but
"What part of me is asking to be free?"
Sometimes the lesson is not to love less,
but to love differently —
from awareness rather than survival.
When the body finally feels safe,
Love no longer feels like danger disguised as desire.
It feels like breathing again.
Sexual Expression and the Body's Intelligence
Desire is not random.
It is the language of the nervous system searching for completion.
When trauma has touched the body, the pathways of pleasure and protection intertwine.
Some people become hyper-responsive—seeking touch, excitement, or intensity as a way to feel alive.
Others shut down, their bodies going numb when closeness appears.
Neither reaction is wrong; both are evidence of a body that learned to survive.
Neuroscience shows that sexual arousal and fear share overlapping circuitry.
The amygdala—the same brain region that signals danger—also influences desire.
This is why some people feel aroused when power dynamics appear, or why calm intimacy feels unfamiliar.
The body confuses *activation* with *aliveness*.
Understanding this frees us from shame.
Arousal patterns are not moral statements; they are memory pathways.
When you begin to notice them without judgment, curiosity replaces guilt, and curiosity is the first form of healing.

Dominance and Submission — Power as Language
Power dynamics are among humanity's oldest erotic symbols.
They can represent danger or devotion, fear or freedom.
Their meaning depends on the consciousness behind them.
For some, dominance arises from a childhood where control was impossible.
Leading becomes a way to stay grounded.

For others, submission is the deepest relief—the first time responsibility can rest.

When practiced consciously, both can be sacred: one gives structure, the other gives surrender.

Problems arise only when these roles are driven by unconscious pain rather than choice.

When dominance hides fear of vulnerability, or submission masks fear of rejection, the body repeats old stories instead of writing new ones.

Healthy erotic power is not about hierarchy.

It is about trust.

It asks: *Can I hold or be held without losing myself?*

When the answer is yes, the dynamic becomes art rather than reenactment.

Body Image, Shame and Presence

Trauma often teaches the body to disappear.

If the body once felt unsafe, it learns invisibility as protection.

But in intimacy, invisibility becomes loneliness.

Many survivors struggle to be seen, touched, or even to meet their own reflection.

Shame lives in muscle memory.

It whispers that pleasure is undeserved or dangerous.

This shame is not personal—it is inherited from moments when the body was treated without reverence.

The path home is gentle re-embodiment.

To feel sensation without story.

To let the body become a friend again rather than an enemy to fix.

Somatic therapies and mindful touch exercises help rebuild this trust; so do simple practices—breathing, movement, dancing, bathing with awareness.

You do not have to love your body immediately.

You only have to stop abandoning it.

Vulnerability, Trust and the Window of Tolerance

In intimacy, emotions rise faster than logic.

The nervous system can tip beyond its *window of tolerance*—the range where feelings are manageable.

Outside it, the body floods with adrenaline or shuts down to preserve energy.

Learning to widen this window is the foundation of relational healing.

It happens through repetition of safe moments: steady eye contact, slow breathing, honesty received without punishment.

Each time safety is proven rather than promised, the nervous system rewrites its code.

Trust is not the absence of fear; it is the willingness to stay present while fear softens.

Love matures when two people can hold discomfort without fleeing it.

This is not romantic idealism—it is neuroplasticity in action.

The brain learns through experience that connection and danger no longer mean the same thing.

Integration — When Awareness Meets Compassion

Healing sexual wounds does not require erasing desire.

It asks for understanding.

When you ask, "Does this impulse come from freedom or fear?" you step into conscious intimacy.

From there, you can keep what feels true and release what feels protective.

Desire becomes integrated rather than divided.

Safe relationships—romantic or otherwise—become laboratories of new experience.

Patience, transparency, and mutual regulation slowly replace the old circuitry of panic and withdrawal.

Pleasure stops being escaped and becomes communion.

Remember: you do not need to be "normal."

You need to be *authentic*.

Whatever your pattern—dominant, submissive, passionate, tender, bold, shy—when it is met with awareness, it becomes expression instead of repetition.

Sexuality is not brokenness trying to be fixed; it is life trying to feel itself again.

Spiritual Meaning:

The body seeks not only pleasure but peace.

It longs to merge what was once divided—fear and desire, power and surrender, safety and passion.

When you meet your own longing with compassion instead of shame, every part of you returns to wholeness.

Quote:

"You are not strange for what you desire.

You are sacred for being honest about it."

Healing Practice:

Find a quiet space.

Sit or lie comfortably.

Bring to mind a moment of desire that once confused or shamed you.

Breathe slowly and whisper:

"I understand why you learned this.

You were surviving.

You can relax now."

Notice what softens—maybe the breath, maybe the chest, maybe the story.

Do nothing else.

Awareness itself is the repair.

12.2 — The Physiology of Intimacy

(Where the Body Learns to Trust Again)

Before touch, there is sensing.

Before desire, there is safety.

Before arousal, there is permission.

Intimacy begins long before skin meets skin.

It begins in the silent conversation between two nervous systems, each scanning for one question:

"Am I safe to open?"

Our biology speaks this language fluently, even when our minds pretend otherwise. The heart rate synchronizes with another's breath; the pupils dilate in microseconds of recognition; the vagus nerve sends quiet signals that say *approach* or *protect*.

Every intimate moment is therefore not just emotional — it is neurological. The body does not distinguish between a lover's gaze and a potential threat until it learns how to. Healing intimacy requires re-teaching the body what safety feels like.

The Body's Ancient Alarm

When trauma has lived in the system, the autonomic nervous network becomes tuned to detect danger faster than it detects love. A gentle gesture may trigger the same alarm once reserved for harm. This isn't brokenness; it is precision — the body remembering too well.

In this state, closeness can spark both longing and fear.

The heart races, not from passion but from vigilance.

The muscles brace for an impact that never comes.

This is what trauma specialists call nervous-system dysregulation: a body oscillating between tension and numbness, between fight and freeze, never fully landing in rest. It's why love can feel too much and silence can feel unsafe.

Relearning safety is not intellectual.

It's a slow recalibration — the way a musician re-tunes an instrument that's been strung too tight for years.

The Narrow Gate of Tolerance

Therapists describe an invisible threshold called the window of tolerance — the zone where our emotions remain intense but manageable. Within this space, the body can feel, process, and stay connected.

When intimacy pushes us beyond that window, we may spiral into two directions:

Hyperarousal, where anxiety and impulse flood the system; or

Hypoarousal, where sensation dims and presence fades.

The aim of healing is not to avoid intensity, but to widen that window so the body can hold passion without panic, closeness without collapse. Breathwork, grounding, movement, and co-regulation — the rhythm of two calm bodies breathing together — gently stretch this capacity. Over time, the body begins to trust that it can stay awake in pleasure without losing control.

Attachment in the Body, Not Just the Mind

While attachment theory often focuses on emotion and behavior, its roots are biological. Long before words like "anxious" or "avoidant," the infant's body learned to regulate through touch, tone, and timing. The heart and the breath found rhythm through the caregiver's presence — or lost it through absence.

In adulthood, that same imprint surfaces in intimacy.

The anxious body moves closer to stay connected.

The avoidant body moves away to feel safe.

The disorganized body does both at once.

Healing does not erase these patterns; it gives them new choreography. When partners practice awareness rather than reaction — pausing, naming sensations, holding eye contact through discomfort — the nervous system receives updated information: "Closeness can happen, and I remain intact."

This is the neurobiology of trust.

The Safety Paradox

Ironically, many survivors find that peace feels more unsettling than chaos.

When nothing is wrong, the body wonders what it has missed.

Stillness can sound like danger when noise was once normal.

This paradox is not self-sabotage. It's simply that the nervous system has equated alertness with survival. True healing therefore means learning to endure calm — to stay present even when no crisis demands attention.

The practice is subtle: noticing the quiet, breathing through it, and letting stillness become familiar rather than foreign. Eventually, the absence of danger begins to register as safety, not suspense.

Desire as a Nervous System Event

Arousal isn't only sexual — it's a state of activation.

The same chemistry that fuels fear also fuels desire: adrenaline, dopamine, oxytocin.

The difference lies in context. When safety is missing, arousal can feel like panic. When safety is present, that same energy becomes pleasure.

This is why healing intimacy must involve the whole body. Pleasure cannot be forced; it unfolds when the system no longer confuses intensity with risk. The more a person learns to stay connected to their breath, their heartbeat, their ground, the more erotic energy transforms from chaos into coherence.

In this way, sexual healing is nervous-system healing.

The goal is not excitement — it's integration.

Presence as Medicine

No partner can heal another, but presence can invite regulation.

When someone breathes slowly beside you, maintains a soft gaze, or waits instead of reaching, the body receives a new template: connection without pressure.

That repetition — gentle, steady, consistent — is what rewires the circuits of intimacy.

Over time, touch no longer means intrusion.

Eye contact no longer feels like exposure.

Desire no longer demands defense.

Safety has become embodied truth.

Spiritual Reflection

The nervous system is not only a biological network; it is also the bridge between soul and flesh.

Each heartbeat is a conversation between the finite and the eternal.

When you breathe with awareness, you're not just calming your body — you're aligning with the rhythm of life itself.

As Rumi wrote,

"There is a voice that doesn't use words. Listen."

That voice is your body.

And it has always been speaking.

Healing Practice

Find a quiet space. Sit comfortably.

Inhale through the nose for four counts, exhale through the mouth for six.

Place a hand on your chest and another on your lower belly.

Whisper softly:

"It's safe to feel.

It's safe to stay.

I am here."

Continue until your body sighs — that small exhale of surrender — the signal that safety has entered the room.

12.3 — Power and Surrender

(The Dance Between Control and Trust)
There is a quiet truth about intimacy that few speak of:
we do not fear losing others — we fear losing ourselves within them.
Power and surrender live at that edge.
They are not opposites.
They are two halves of the same breath — the inhale of strength, the exhale of trust.
When one is out of balance, connection collapses into control.
When both are honored, intimacy becomes an act of awareness.

The Nature of Power

Power, in its purest form, is not dominance — it is presence.

It is the ability to remain grounded while holding another's vulnerability with reverence.

It is knowing your own energy so well that you can meet others without collapsing or overpowering.

Healthy power does not need to be proven.
It listens. It holds. It guides.
In the body, power feels like groundedness — feet rooted, chest open, breath steady. It's not about being "on top," but about being inside your own integrity while inviting another to do the same.

Psychologically, this kind of power arises from secure boundaries. The nervous system feels safe enough to stay open. It can lead without forcing, decide without defending, act without aggression.

Power, then, becomes a form of containment — a space where energy can move freely without chaos.

The Nature of Surrender

Surrender is not submission.
It is not weakness, nor passivity.
It is the art of softening in the presence of safety.
Where power says, "I will hold," surrender whispers, "I trust you enough to let go."
True surrender is a conscious act.
It requires strength to release control — a strength that can only come from deep self-awareness.

Surrender begins in the nervous system: the muscles unclench, the breath deepens, the body says, *"I am not in danger anymore."*
When surrender is coerced, it becomes trauma.
When surrender is chosen, it becomes transcendence.

Power and Surrender in the Body

From a neurobiological view, both power and surrender engage the autonomic nervous system, the body's regulation center.

Power activates the sympathetic branch — energy rising, focus sharpening, heart quickening.

Surrender activates the parasympathetic branch — release, softness, expansion, connection.

When both coexist harmoniously, the body enters a state of coherence: alert and relaxed at once. This is the physiological signature of flow — the same state artists, athletes, and lovers describe when time disappears.

That balance — alert yet open — is not achieved through force.

It is cultivated through presence.

Presence is the meeting point between control and letting go.

The Psychology of Power Dynamics

In intimacy, power is inevitable. Someone initiates, someone receives. Someone leads, someone follows. This polarity is not inequality; it is energy in motion.

When trauma remains unhealed, power becomes distorted — used to avoid vulnerability or to reenact old helplessness. One might dominate to feel safe, or submit to avoid conflict.

But when power is conscious, it transforms into creative tension — a sacred polarity that heightens awareness rather than fear.

The question is not, *"Who has control?"*

The real question is, *"Is control being shared or defended?"*

Healthy dynamics are fluid: both partners able to lead or yield in rhythm, aware of choice at every moment.

Unhealthy dynamics are rigid: one remains frozen in defense while the other holds unspoken authority.

Conscious relationships thrive in movement.

Rigidity is the symptom of unhealed fear.

The Paradox of Safety and Risk

Love and sexuality always hold a paradox — we must risk to feel alive.

Too much control, and the soul suffocates.

Too much surrender, and the self dissolves.

Intimacy lives in between — the thin line where self-awareness and openness meet.

It is not about eliminating risk; it is about creating containers where risk becomes exploration, not threat.

Boundaries do not cage desire.

They shape it.

As the mystic poet Kahlil Gibran wrote:

"Let there be spaces in your togetherness."

That space — that breath between two — is where power and surrender can dance without fear of loss.

The Science of Safety in Surrender

Dr. Stephen Porges' research shows that true safety activates the social engagement system — facial muscles soften, voice tones warm, heartbeats synchronize. In that state, both partners' vagus nerves communicate ease to one another.

When this happens, surrender becomes possible because the body recognizes: *"I am safe to open."*

Safety is not just emotional reassurance — it is physiological permission.

When someone feels seen, not judged; held, not handled; met, not managed — the body naturally lets go.

This is not performance; this is co-regulation — the nervous system's ancient way of saying, "We belong."

The Energy of Polarity

Tantric philosophy teaches that every human carries both receptive and directive energies — often symbolized as feminine and masculine, though neither are bound by gender.

The feminine energy moves like water: fluid, emotional, expressive, intuitive.

The masculine energy moves like fire: focused, steady, directional, witnessing.

When these energies meet in awareness, the body becomes an instrument of balance — flow and structure, motion and stillness, giving and receiving.

Pleasure expands beyond the physical; it becomes a presence in motion.

Polarity isn't about roles or stereotypes — it's about rhythm.

One leads so the other can let go. Then they switch, without fear of losing identity.

In this way, power and surrender stop being roles and become mutual offerings.

Spiritual Reflection: The Sacred Exchange

To truly meet another, you must risk being changed.

That is the quiet truth behind all intimacy — not the loss of self, but the evolution of it.

When power is held with awareness and surrender is offered with trust, a third presence appears — something larger than both. Some call it God, others love, others consciousness itself.

It is the same stillness monks find in prayer and dancers find in movement — the moment the self becomes both giver and receiver, both lover and beloved.

Power says, *"I hold you."*
Surrender says, *"I trust you."*
Spirit says, *"You are one."*

12.4 — Conscious Sexuality and Shadow Integration

(Where Light and Darkness Learn to Dance)

Every person carries two landscapes within them — the one they show the world, and the one that breathes in secret.

The outer world speaks in politeness, restraint, and performance.

The inner world whispers in hunger, imagination, and memory.

Conscious sexuality is not about choosing one over the other.

It is about uniting them — bringing the hidden into light, not to control it, but to understand it.

Because what we hide does not disappear.

It waits.

And it rules from the shadows until it is met with love.

The Shadow of Desire

Desire is one of the most misunderstood human forces.

It has been shamed, controlled, moralized, and commercialized — yet it remains one of the purest reflections of our life force.

Carl Jung wrote that "the shadow is everything we refuse to be."

In sexuality, that means the emotions, fantasies, and impulses we judge as *too much, too strange, too dangerous,* or *too shameful.*

But repression does not purify desire — it only drives it underground, where it becomes distorted.

The more we hide what we want, the more it controls us.

The more we meet it with compassion, the more it transforms into insight.

To integrate the shadow is to say, "Nothing human is foreign to me."

It is to look at your desire — even the wild, confusing, forbidden parts — and whisper: *"I see you. You belong."*

The Body as the Mirror of the Unconscious

Sexual energy is not purely physical. It is a language of the unconscious.

The body expresses what the mind cannot say: shame, power, grief, longing, freedom.

In the field of somatic psychology, this is understood as implicit communication — the body re-enacts unspoken emotional stories through touch, posture, breath, and movement.

That's why arousal can feel confusing: the body remembers things the conscious mind has forgotten.

Conscious sexuality invites us to listen rather than react.

When a fantasy arises, instead of judging it, we ask:

"What emotion is this carrying?"

"What part of me is seeking expression?"

A fantasy of control might hide a longing for safety.

A fantasy of surrender might mask exhaustion from holding the world together.

A fantasy of exhibition might be the soul's rebellion against invisibility.

Desire, when decoded with tenderness, becomes self-knowledge.

Shame: The Silent Cage

Shame is the heaviest emotion in human intimacy.

It teaches us that to be desired is dangerous, to be seen is risky, to enjoy is sinful.

But shame is not moral truth — it is inherited conditioning.

Many cultures, especially those shaped by fear-based morality, disconnected sex from spirit — labeling the body as impure and desire as weakness.

Yet across history's deeper layers, ancient traditions told a different story:

the body was the temple, not the obstacle;

pleasure was prayer, not sin;

and the act of union mirrored the dance between creation and consciousness itself.

To heal shame, we must return to this remembrance:

that the sacred and the sensual were never separate.

That divinity moves through flesh, breath, pulse, and presence.

Meeting the Shadow Without Being Consumed

Integration does not mean indulgence.

It means awareness with compassion — holding the dark without letting it dominate.

The goal is not to act out every desire, but to understand its roots.

When we repress, we lose freedom.

When we identify with our impulses, we lose balance.

Integration is the middle path — acknowledging everything, acting from wisdom.

In Jungian terms, this is alchemy: transforming instinct into art, compulsion into choice.

When awareness meets the shadow, the raw energy of desire becomes creativity, passion, and connection.

That transformation is the essence of conscious sexuality:

not the death of desire, but its evolution.

Erotic Intelligence

Psychotherapist Esther Perel describes eroticism as "the antidote to death" — the force that reminds us we are alive.

To be erotic is not merely to seek pleasure; it is to awaken to life's vibrancy.

It is the moment we feel our pulse and know: *I exist, I am here, I am feeling.*

Erotic intelligence is the capacity to hold complexity — to feel pleasure and vulnerability, power and tenderness, desire and fear — without needing to choose one over the other.

In this space, sex becomes more than physical release.

It becomes communion — an act of awareness where two people meet not to escape themselves, but to remember who they are.

The body becomes the instrument of consciousness itself.

Each breath, each touch, each pause becomes a meditation.

This is not fantasy; it is presence made tangible.

The Role of Conscious Partners

Healing through intimacy requires partners who understand that safety is built through attunement, not perfection.

A conscious partner does not perform; they listen.

They understand that consent is not a contract — it's a conversation.

A conscious partner can hold space for the other's tremble, confusion, tears, and joy.

They know that real erotic connection begins after the masks fall — when there is nowhere left to hide, and yet, no need to.

To love consciously is to say:

"I will not use your openness to feed my power.

I will use my presence to feed your freedom."

Integrating Pleasure and Pain

Every human carries a unique emotional blueprint. Some find comfort in intensity; others in gentleness. Some need control to feel alive; others need surrender to feel safe.

Conscious sexuality makes room for all of it — as long as awareness and consent guide the experience.

Pleasure and pain, when explored safely, can mirror the dual nature of life: tension and release, contraction and expansion, birth and death.

To explore this consciously is not perversion — it is courage.

It is to reclaim your body from fear and allow it to speak its own sacred language.

In the end, integration means this:

You are neither the light nor the shadow — you are the whole sky that holds them both.

Spiritual Meaning:

The body is not the opposite of spirit.

It is the doorway into it.

Each sensation, each breath, each heartbeat is the universe speaking your name.

As the mystic poet Lalla wrote in the 14th century:

"I did not know who I was until love burned me and revealed my own reflection."

To walk the path of conscious sexuality is to allow love — not romance, but awakening — to burn through illusion until only truth remains.

Quote:

"When the body finally feels safe, it does not become smaller —
it becomes honest, expressive, alive.
Desire is what emerges when the war inside is over."

Healing Practice:
Tonight, before sleep, place a hand on your chest and another over your lower belly.
Close your eyes and breathe slowly.
Visualize a small flame in your heart.
With every exhale, imagine the flame traveling down to your pelvis — light meeting instinct, soul meeting body.
Whisper:
"I am whole.
My desire is not my enemy.
My shadow is not my shame.
I am safe to feel what is real."
Stay until the breath and heartbeat move as one.
That is integration — the soul remembering its body.

12.5 — Spiritual Union and Integration

(Where Two Become One Without Disappearing)

There is a moment in healing when the body stops defending and starts remembering. A moment when you no longer need to fix what was broken, because you realize — it was never broken, only waiting to be seen through love.

Spiritual union begins here — not in perfection, but in presence.
It is the space where the body and consciousness finally meet, where the human and the divine recognize each other as reflections.

This is not a fairytale of eternal harmony.
It is a lived experience — the pulse, the breath, the trembling, the silence — where the heart remembers that it was never separate from anything.

Union Beyond Possession

In unconscious love, we cling.
We try to own, to hold, to merge until individuality disappears.
In awakened love, we realize: merging does not mean losing — it means *meeting fully while remaining whole.*

The paradox of union is this:
two people can melt into one current of energy, yet remain anchored in their own centers.
This is not dependency; it is resonance.
Each heart becomes a tuning fork that refines the other.

In this kind of love, boundaries do not separate — they define shape.
Like the shore gives form to the sea, boundaries allow energy to move without flooding.

Union, then, is not a loss of self.
It is the awakening of self within the shared field of consciousness.

The Alchemy of Two Nervous Systems

When two people enter intimacy with awareness, their nervous systems begin to co-regulate — heartbeats synchronize, breath patterns align, muscle tension melts in mirrored rhythms.
This is not poetic fantasy; it is measurable neurobiology.

In that resonance, something deeper happens:
the mind softens, the sense of time fades, and presence expands beyond "me" and "you."

This is where science meets spirituality — the nervous system becomes a bridge between body and consciousness.
Every breath exchanged becomes a meditation.
Every touch becomes prayer.
Every silence becomes communion.

This is what Tantra has always pointed to:
union not as performance, but as awakening.

Love as Energy, Not Emotion

Most of us mistake love for a feeling.
But feelings rise and fall; love, as energy, remains constant.

Love is the field in which experience happens.
It is the intelligence that organizes everything into connection — the glue of atoms, the pulse of nature, the silence between heartbeats.

When you are truly present with another, you are not "creating" love — you are remembering the field you already share.

This is why spiritual union feels like coming home: the body recognizes the frequency of belonging.
It is not a dependency. It is resonance returning to its source.

The Practice of Stillness in Intimacy
Stillness is the forgotten language of connection.
In the modern world, we chase intensity — we want fireworks, not the quiet hum of presence.
But the deepest intimacy often unfolds in stillness: the slow breath, the gaze that doesn't flinch, the silence that says, *"I am here."*

Stillness is not absence.
It is fullness.
It is the moment the nervous system feels so safe that nothing needs to happen.

In that stillness, the spiritual and physical merge — the sacred meeting of consciousness with form.
What mystics call "union with the divine" can be felt in the smallest, most human gesture:
a hand resting on another's skin,
a sigh that says, *"I trust you,"*
a moment where nothing needs to be said.

Sex as Prayer, Touch as Presence
When the body becomes conscious, sex transforms into something far beyond sensation.
Each touch becomes a meditation, a dialogue between souls through skin.
Pleasure becomes not just release but revelation — the awareness that the divine lives inside matter.

Tantric traditions describe this as the "sacralization of experience."
It means every act of love — whether physical or emotional — can be holy when entered with awareness.
Not because of ritual, but because of presence.

In that moment, orgasm becomes not an escape but a surrender — the small death of the ego that allows the infinite to breathe through you.
You disappear, yet you have never been more alive.

Transcendence Through Embodiment

Spiritual awakening is not about leaving the body — it is about descending fully into it.
The body is not the obstacle to enlightenment; it is the instrument.
In the heart of intimacy, when awareness stays anchored in sensation, time dissolves, and the illusion of separation fades.
You realize that pleasure and pain, light and dark, giving and receiving — they are all expressions of the same pulse of creation.
This is what mystics meant by *union with the Beloved* —
not an idea, but a felt experience of oneness moving through two forms.
When you awaken through the body, spirituality stops being philosophy and becomes biology infused with divinity.

Integration: The Afterglow of Awareness

Every transcendent moment must eventually return to earth.
Integration means carrying the awareness of union into daily life —
how you speak, how you touch, how you listen.
After the merging, come back to your own breath.
After the ecstasy, tend to the ordinary.
That is where enlightenment matures — not in escape, but in embodiment.
The question is not "How do I stay transcendent?"
but "How do I love the world from this new depth of presence?"
Integration is how divinity becomes lived humanity.
It is how we turn mystical experience into kindness, compassion, and art.

Spiritual Meaning:

Union is not the end of longing; it is the beginning of belonging.
When two awaken together, they do not rise above the world — they bless it by their presence.

HEALING INTIMACY

Love, at its highest form, is consciousness remembering itself through touch, through laughter, through the quiet miracle of being human.

As the poet Hafiz said:

"The sun never says to the earth, 'You owe me.'
Look what happens with a love like that —
it lights the whole sky."

Quote:

"Your erotic self is not a shadow of your trauma;

it is the part of you that survived it.

Treat it not as a wound to correct,

but as a doorway back to your wholeness."

Chapter 13
Love After Awakening

13.1 — When the Eternal Meets the Everyday

The Moment Everything Changes

There's this moment when everything just... stops.
    All the noise in your head goes quiet, and suddenly you see through all the stories you've been telling yourself.
You're not your thoughts.
You're not even the name people call you.
You're the space that holds it all—silent, huge, awake.
    For a breath, it feels like pure freedom.
You've touched something beyond fear or needing anything.
You've seen that you were never really separate from life itself.
It feels like finally coming home.
    Then morning comes.

Someone asks what's for breakfast.
Your phone buzzes.
Someone you love needs your attention.
The infinite is being asked to take out the trash.

And that's when the real journey begins.

How do you live as this vast awareness inside a life that still has dirty dishes, complicated feelings, and other people with their own stuff going on?

When the Light Hits Real Life

Awakening shows you that everything is connected—that we're all one.

But love? Love happens between two people.

You might remember that deep peace you felt, but here you are sharing space with another person who has moods, baggage, and their own needs.

It gets confusing.

You've touched eternity, but someone's tone of voice still hurts.
You've felt God, but you still get jealous or lonely.
You've seen the truth, but you still react like a kid sometimes.

Some people deal with this by pulling away. They say, *"I've outgrown this relationship stuff."*

Others hide behind spiritual talk to avoid the pain: *"It's just ego, it doesn't really matter."*

But avoiding the hurt only makes it louder.

Awakening was never meant to take you out of life.
It was meant to take you deeper into it.

When Spiritual Becomes a Shield

When awakening first happens, your mind can turn it into armor.

You tell yourself, *"I don't need anyone anymore."*

You call distance "detachment" and numbness "clarity."

But peace that needs you to stay away from people isn't real peace—it's just protection.

Real awakening softens you.

It doesn't make you float above your feelings—it lets you feel everything without drowning.

It doesn't close your heart—it makes your heart big enough to hold the whole messy world.

The proof of awakening isn't how long you can sit in silence.
It's how kindly you can live.

Two Worlds, One Heart

The old teachers talked about two kinds of truth:

The absolute truth: Everything is one. There's no separation. You're pure awareness—eternal, untouchable, free.

The everyday truth: You and I are here as two separate people. We have conversations. We have conflicts. We hurt each other and repair. We're human.

Both are real.

If you only focus on the absolute, you forget you're human.
If you only focus on the everyday, you forget you're divine.

Awakening asks you to live in both.

To remember the sky while you're walking on earth.
To see God in the human mess—and the human mess as holy.

When you bring that deep stillness into daily life, ordinary things start to glow.

A look. A word. A meal together—each one becomes a doorway back to truth.

Belonging to Yourself

Before awakening, most of us looked for belonging outside ourselves.

We wanted to be chosen, needed, told we were enough.

We tried to hold people close so the emptiness inside would finally be quiet.

But belonging you get by holding on never lasts.
It slips away the second someone pulls back.

After awakening, belonging starts to grow inside you.

You realize you don't have to earn your place in the world.
You belong because you're breathing.
Because life itself is breathing you.

When that truth settles into your body—not just your head—everything relaxes.

Your shoulders drop.
Your breath gets easier.
And love stops feeling like a race you have to win. It becomes a rhythm you join.

The Lonely Part Nobody Talks About

There's often this silence that comes after the light.

You see things differently now, and not everyone sees it with you.

Old conversations feel shallow.

Old goals lose their shine.

Even people you love can feel far away, like you're speaking different languages.

This can feel like loneliness. And it is. But it's not emptiness—*it's space.*

The space where the old you dissolves so something truer can show up.

Sit with it.

Let it stretch you.

Let it teach you how to be with yourself without needing someone else to make it okay.

Loneliness becomes sacred when you stop running from it.

It turns into openness. And in that openness, love quietly comes back—not as neediness, but as simple presence.

Learning to Stay

Love after awakening asks for one main thing: **staying.**

Staying in your body when emotion rises.

Staying in the room when it gets uncomfortable.

Staying with your own heart when it wants to run.

Each time you stay, your nervous system learns something new:

That closeness isn't dangerous.

That being tender isn't weak.

That you can be open and still be okay.

Staying doesn't mean clinging.

It means you stop abandoning yourself.

You're home in yourself, wherever you are.

The Beauty of Simple Things

The awakened life isn't about dramatic experiences or constant bliss.

It's about doing simple things with your full attention.

Washing dishes slowly.

Listening without trying to fix anything.

Feeling sunlight on your face and realizing—this is God too.

Love starts to feel like that.

Not fireworks. Just a steady warmth.
Not constant excitement. Just deep comfort.
Not needing to prove anything. Just being together.

You start to see that peace was never about escaping the world.
It was about seeing the world clearly—and loving it anyway.

Being Kind to Your Human Parts

Even after awakening, old patterns show up.

Fear knocks on your door.

You compare yourself to others.

You want to be seen and chosen.

These aren't failures.

They're the places where more light wants to get in.

Instead of fighting them, you start to listen.

You breathe with the fear.

You sit next to the loneliness.

You talk gently to the kid inside who still wants to be loved.

Healing now isn't about fixing yourself.

It's about welcoming all of yourself.

When you can hold your own messy, human parts with kindness, it becomes natural to hold other people that way too.

And love gets safer, because nothing in you has to hide anymore.

Coming Back to Life

Awakening isn't an escape from the world.

It's the return to it—with your eyes open and your heart unguarded.

You still pay bills. You still make dinner. You still mess up sometimes.

But something has changed.

You act from love, not from lack.

You move slower. Breathe deeper. Listen longer.

You realize enlightenment was never about living alone on a mountain.

It was meant to be lived through kindness, through presence, through the way you touch everyday life.

The divine doesn't just live in temples or meditation cushions.
It lives in how gently you talk to your partner when you're both tired.
It lives in how patiently you wait when someone's struggling.
It lives in how real you're willing to be.
Enlightenment isn't about becoming more spiritual.

It's about becoming more real.

The Holy in the Ordinary
Here's the turn that happens on the spiritual path:
You start out looking for something higher—some escape from pain, some freedom from being human.
And you end up falling in love with ordinary life.
The way light comes through a window.
The sound of someone you love breathing in their sleep.
The taste of morning coffee. The feeling of bare feet on grass.
The holy act of just showing up, day after day, to this simple, beautiful, difficult life.
The poet Mary Oliver asked:
"Tell me, what is it you plan to do with your one wild and precious life?"
After awakening, the answer gets simple:
Love what's here.
Be present for what shows up.
Take care of your own heart so it can be a safe place for others.
Live so fully human that the divine shines through everything you do.

This is what it all comes down to:
Awakening doesn't take you somewhere else.
It brings you home—to this breath, this moment, this love, this life.
And when you finally come home, you discover what the wise ones always knew:
The sacred and the ordinary were never different things.
Heaven isn't a place you go to. It's who you become.
And love—real love—happens when you stop hiding from your own light.

Spiritual Meaning:

Awakening is not the end of your human story.

It is the beginning of living it with open eyes and an open heart.

Quote:

"The proof of awakening is not in silence, but in gentleness."

Healing Practice:

Take a slow breath in.

Feel your chest rise and fall.

Whisper,

"I am both the sky and the soil."

Let the words settle, reminding you that you can be vast and human, infinite and tender, all at once.

13.2 — Relearning Belonging: From Seeking to Wholeness

When the wave remembers it is the ocean, something inside begins to rest.

But rest does not mean stillness forever.

The wave still moves, still meets the shore, still feels the pull of the moon.

Awakening does not erase our humanness.

It invites us to meet it with tenderness.

We begin again — not as someone lost, but as someone found.

Belonging Begins in the Body

Before awakening, many of us searched for belonging outside ourselves.

We tried to earn it through love, through approval, through being good enough or spiritual enough.

We shaped our voices to be accepted.

We dimmed our light to keep the peace.

We said yes when our hearts whispered no.

And for a while, it worked — or at least, it seemed to.

We felt safe when someone praised us, seen when someone chose us.

But the comfort never lasted long.

We were always waiting for the next sign that we mattered.

After awakening, this search begins to soften.

You start to see that belonging isn't something you get — it's something you remember.

You belong because you exist.

Because the same life breathing through the trees is breathing through you.

When you let that truth touch your heart, your body starts to relax.

The shoulders drop.

The breath deepens.

The world, for the first time, feels like home.

The Loneliness That Comes Before Union

There is a strange and quiet loneliness that comes after awakening.

It is not the loneliness of missing someone.

It is the loneliness of realizing that no one and nothing can fill you — because you were never truly empty.

This can feel like a loss at first.

The old joys fall silent; the familiar identities fade.

You may look at your partner and wonder why everything feels different.

You may look at yourself and wonder who you are now.

But loneliness is not a punishment.

It is the clearing before true connection.

It is the sacred pause where the old ways of relating dissolve, and a new kind of love begins to form.

To belong after awakening, you must first belong to the silence inside.

To the breath that asks for nothing.

To the stillness that is not waiting for applause.

In that space, love finds you again — not as need, but as presence.

Relationship as a Mirror of Return

When you start to live from this quiet center, every relationship changes.

The people closest to you no longer exist to complete you — they exist to reflect you.

Each person you meet becomes a mirror, showing the places you still protect, the tenderness you still withhold, the light you haven't yet dared to shine.

Sometimes that mirror feels gentle and loving.

Sometimes it feels harsh and uncomfortable.

Either way, it is sacred.

A partner's silence might reveal your old fear of being ignored.

Their closeness might awaken your fear of losing yourself.

Their anger might call forth your own hidden rage.

Their love might expose how much you still resist being loved.

Awakening does not mean these triggers disappear.

It means you stop running from them.

You begin to see them as invitations:

to breathe,

to soften,

to meet what is rising with curiosity instead of judgment.

This is how awakening becomes embodied — through relationships.

Through the small, daily acts of staying present when the old self wants to flee.

The New Way of Loving

When love no longer comes from need, it becomes gentle.

You start to love not because you want something, but because loving feels true.

It becomes less about "What can I get?" and more about "What can I give while still remaining whole?"

This love does not rush.

It does not perform.

It does not demand perfection.

It breathes with patience.

It listens without preparing an answer.

It honors differences without fear.

It holds space for both silence and laughter.

To love this way, you must stay connected to yourself.

Otherwise, you slip back into the old pattern of disappearing to keep peace.

So you learn to check in, quietly:

"Am I here?"

"Am I grounded?"

"Am I giving from fullness or from fear?"

When you start asking these questions, love becomes clear again — not something fragile you must protect, but something vast you can trust.

Awakened Love Is Ordinary

Many people imagine awakened love as fireworks or cosmic bliss.

But in truth, it often looks very simple.

It is the kindness of folding the blanket at night.

It is the patience of waiting while someone finds their words.

It is the courage to say, "I was wrong."

The awakened heart does not need drama to feel alive.

It finds beauty in the quiet gestures that say, *I see you.*

It finds holiness in the hand reaching across the table.

When consciousness touches the ordinary, the ordinary becomes sacred.

When love meets awareness, the whole world becomes prayer.

Meeting the Unawakened with Grace

Sometimes, the person you love has not shared your awakening.

You may feel worlds apart — one seeing the sky from the mountaintop, the other still in the valley.

But the truth is: both are sacred paths.

If you believe you are "more evolved," the heart closes.

If you look down from your light, you lose the warmth that makes it shine.

Remember: awakening is not superiority — it is responsibility.

You have seen unity; now you are asked to live it.

To bring compassion into the ordinary.

To meet your partner where they are — with patience, curiosity, and respect.

This is not lowering your vibration.

It is embodying it.

It is making the divine practical, human, touchable.

As Marianne Williamson said,

"The spiritual journey is not about transcending our humanity, but bringing our humanity into alignment with our divinity."

The Art of Staying Open

To stay open after awakening takes courage.

When you no longer hide behind need or fantasy, you feel more deeply.

Love touches every nerve.

The heart trembles — not from weakness, but from aliveness.

You learn that true intimacy is not about two people merging; it is about two souls standing side by side, transparent and free.

You stop trying to control the outcome.

You begin to trust the unfolding.

Sometimes that unfolding means staying.

Sometimes it means letting go.

Either way, love remains — not as possession, but as presence.

Emptiness and Form

As your heart opens, you start to see that love is not opposite to emptiness — it is born from it.

The more you rest in silence, the more love flows naturally.

It doesn't depend on effort.

It doesn't depend on who stays or goes.

It moves like sunlight — shining because it cannot help but shine.

To love after awakening is to live as that light.

To care deeply without trying to control.

To give without losing yourself.

To hold another close while knowing that both of you belong to something infinite.

This is the new belonging — not ownership, but participation in the great rhythm of life.

Belonging Together, Belonging to All

When two awakened hearts meet, relationship becomes less about "you and me" and more about "us and life."

You begin to sense a shared field of being — a space between you that is alive, breathing, sacred.

You can feel it in the pauses.

In the quiet between words.

In the way your nervous systems start to mirror calm instead of chaos.

This space is not something you create; it is something you allow.

It appears when both hearts rest in honesty.

Here, belonging is not dependency — it is communion.

You belong *with* each other because you already belong *in* life.

Relearning to Receive

One of the final lessons after awakening is learning to receive again.

For so long, you may have survived by giving — by taking care, fixing, healing, teaching.

But now the soul asks: *Can you also let yourself be loved?*

To receive is to trust.

To trust that you are safe.

To trust that you are worthy.

To trust that love is not a transaction, but a circulation.

When you let love move both ways, relationship becomes balanced.

The flow of giving and receiving creates harmony, like breath — inhale and exhale, both sacred.

The Gentle Practice

Belonging after awakening is not something you figure out once.

It is a practice — quiet, daily, lived.

It happens in moments:

when you breathe through a misunderstanding instead of closing;

when you choose to listen instead of defend;

when you place a hand on your heart and remind yourself, *I am safe to stay.*

Each small act of presence rewrites the story of love.

Each breath tells the body: *We are home now.*

Closing Reflection

To belong after awakening is to love without armor.

It is to remember that the divine hides inside the human, waiting to be touched.
It is to live with both feet in the world and your heart in eternity.
You do not need to reach for enlightenment anymore.
You are it — folding laundry, listening, forgiving, laughing, beginning again.
The universe is not asking you to be perfect.
It is asking you to be here.
Fully, tenderly, truthfully — in this sacred moment of being human.

Spiritual Meaning:
Belonging after awakening is remembering that you were never lost — only learning how to stay present to love.

Quote:
"Belonging isn't where you are understood. It's where you no longer need to explain."

Healing Practice:
Sit quietly.
Place both hands over your heart.
Inhale gently through your nose, exhale softly through your mouth.
Whisper,
"I already belong."
Let the breath carry those words through your whole body until you feel them settle like light.

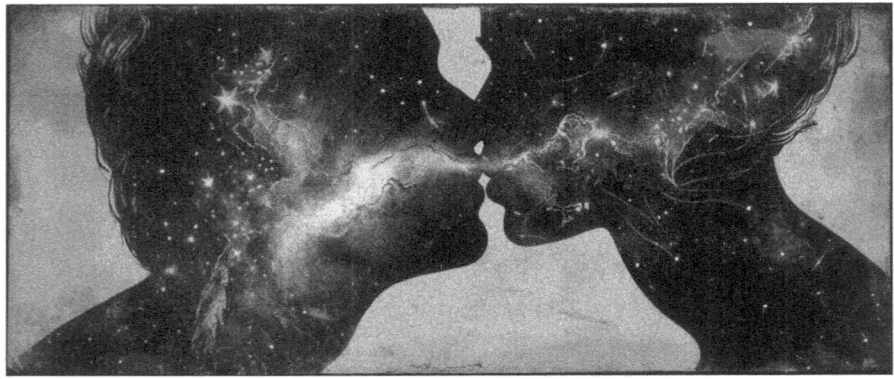

LOVE AFTER AWAKENING

Prelude

– The Quiet Between Worlds

Before love becomes simple again,

it often breaks us open.

We awaken not in a temple, but in the ache of our own heart.

Light pours in through the cracks we once called failure.

The divine whispers: belong here too.

In this ordinary body, in these trembling hands,

in the eyes of the one who meets you halfway —

love waits, not as a dream to chase,

but as the quiet truth that never left.

-Author

PART IV Integration

The gentle return to wholeness there comes a point in every journey

when healing stops being something

we do and begins to become the way we live.

We have traced the body's maps, listened to its memory, and met the shadows that once hid beneath the skin

Now the work softens. It is less about searching, more about allowing.

We are no longer climbing toward light.

We are remembering that we are the light —

learning to carry it in ordinary moments:

when we sip tea, fold a towel,

listen to a friend, breathe before speaking.

Integration is not a final arrival.

It is the art of being whole in motion.

It is where the sacred meets the simple—

where touch becomes prayer,

Stillness becomes song, and life itself becomes the teacher.

Here, love is not rescue.

It is recognition.

Here, healing is not effort.

It is embodiment.

Welcome to the quiet after the storm.

Welcome home to yourself.

-Author

Chapter 14
Rituals for a Soft Life

"A soft life is not the absence of challenge.
It is the end of fighting yourself.
It is living the way a feather moves with air—
unforced, unheld, guided, open."

— Author

A Life Your Nervous System Can Rest Inside

There were mornings when getting out of bed felt impossible.
Not because the world outside was too heavy,
but because the world inside was.

That heaviness was not laziness or weakness.
It was the body whispering, *"I'm still carrying yesterday."*

For years, you may have called this exhaustion, burnout, or depression.
But what if it was something wiser—
your nervous system saying, *"I'm tired of surviving."*

Healing begins in the smallest mornings—
the ones when you wake and, for the first time,
your breath arrives before your thoughts.
You notice the light without flinching.
You meet the day rather than defend against it.
That is where softness starts.

The Morning as a Mirror

Mornings speak the truth the mind tries to hide.
When waking feels like bracing for impact,
your body is still living in yesterday's battlefield.

Each reaction tells a story:

Anxiety – a body already running before you stand.

Numbness – a body that learned to disappear.

Exhaustion – a system running on empty.

Overwhelm – too many unprocessed emotions crowding the doorway.

Your body is not disobedient; it's loyal.
It remembers every moment it needed to stay alert.
When it finally begins to trust again,
you'll feel it — in the ease of your shoulders,
in the way breath finds you without effort,
in the stillness that doesn't scare you anymore.

The Language of the Nervous System

Safety isn't a mantra.
It's physiology.
Dr. Stephen Porges, in his polyvagal work, describes safety
as a state where the body can rest, digest, and connect.
The heart rate slows. The breath deepens.
The gut begins to hum in harmony with the mind.

When we live in survival mode,
the body forgets that rhythm.
It holds its breath waiting for permission to exist.

The soft life is the art of remembering that rhythm—
through slow meals, steady breath,
and the choice not to rush the moment that asks to unfold.

You don't have to force relaxation.
You simply create the space
where relaxation can find you.

Slowness as Medicine

In a world that praises speed, slowness feels rebellious.
But slowness is not laziness; it's biology.

When the body moves slower,
the parasympathetic system — the "rest and digest" network — activates.
Blood flows back to the organs.
The heartbeat steadies.
The mind stops scanning for danger.

This is why monks begin their day with breath,
why yoga opens with stillness,
why children calm when rocked at a gentle rhythm.

Slowness is how life finds its natural tempo again.

Move without urgency.
Eat without tension.
Listen without planning your reply.
These are not luxuries.
They are acts of regulation — tiny rituals that tell the body,
"You are safe now."

Tending the Gut, Tending the Soul

Peace begins in the body long before it reaches the mind.
And one of its quietest gateways is the gut —
the garden where both nourishment and calm begin to grow.

Science tells us that around 90 to 95 percent of the body's serotonin —
the neurotransmitter that steadies mood, supports sleep,
and restores emotional balance — is produced not in the brain,
but in the gut.

This discovery, first illuminated by researchers such as Dr. Elaine Hsiao
at Caltech and UCLA, reminds us that the body's wisdom runs deep —
that healing often begins below the neck.

Yet there's something many people don't realize:
the serotonin in your gut and the serotonin in your brain
are two different systems,
each with its own sacred purpose.

Gut serotonin governs digestion, immunity, and gut rhythm.

Brain serotonin shapes emotion, mood, and thought.

They cannot cross the blood-brain barrier,
but they are in constant communication
through the gut–brain axis —
a shimmering bridge carried by the vagus nerve, immune signals,
and the living intelligence of gut microbes.

When this dialogue is harmonious,
you feel balanced, centered, calm.
When it is disrupted — by stress, inflammation, or neglect —
the mind begins to mirror the chaos of the body.

So nourishing your gut is not vanity;
It is spiritual maintenance.
It's how the body whispers peace back into the mind.

Your gut is not just an organ; it's an ecosystem.
It's home to trillions of tiny allies
that digest, repair, and signal safety to your brain.
They help create tryptophan —
the building block your brain transforms into serotonin —
and through that, they quietly shape how you experience love, rest, and joy.

When your gut is cared for, your whole being becomes more resilient.
The brain rewires more easily, learning new emotional patterns.
Serotonin works alongside a growth molecule called BDNF(Brain-Derived Neurotrophic Factor),
which helps neurons grow and form new connections —
the physical evidence of healing.

In simple words:
a nourished body makes a teachable mind.
A calm gut allows a gentle heart.
Peace in the belly becomes peace in the soul.

So feed yourself as if feeding a sacred garden.
Warm meals, steady rhythms, quiet gratitude before eating —
These small rituals tell your body: *"You are safe now. You can rest."*

This isn't about restrictions or rules.
It's about reverence.
When you eat slowly, you tell life itself,
"I am here. I will not rush this gift."

Imagine soup simmering on the stove —
that gentle heat is a ceremony.
A cup of tea in your hands is a meditation.
The scent of real food, made with love, becomes a kind of prayer.

Before you eat, pause.
Place your hand on your belly.
Whisper softly, *"Thank you for carrying me through."*

In that moment, your body and spirit begin to align —
and the ancient intelligence within you, both scientific and sacred,
remembers what it means to live in harmony again.

The Dopamine Trap

The soft life cannot bloom in a mind constantly chased by reward.
We live in what Dr. Anna Lembke calls the *Dopamine Nation*—
a world addicted to "next":
next message, next scroll, next purchase, next rush.

The nervous system is overstimulated and under-held.
It has forgotten how to feel safe doing nothing.
Silence feels too loud.
Stillness feels too strange.
And so we reach — for phones, for plans, for performance.
But these impulses are not failure;
They are signals of longing.
The body is searching for safety and connection
in the only ways it knows.
When you begin to slow, it will protest.
It will call you restless, bored, even lonely.
Stay anyway.
That is the moment your healing starts.
You are not broken for craving stimulation.
You are simply someone whose system adapted to chaos.
Peace will feel unnatural — until it doesn't.

The Practice of Presence
Presence doesn't arrive through mastery.
It arrives through moment-to-moment mercy.
You pause instead of escape.
You breathe instead of distract.
You stay with yourself for ten seconds longer than before.
That's all it takes — one breath of self-companionship.
Tomorrow morning, when you wake and feel the urge to scroll,
place your hand on your chest instead.
Feel the warmth of your own presence.
That is you returning home.
This small ritual teaches the body:
"I can be with myself and still be safe."
It rebuilds trust not through control,
but through consistency and kindness.

The Philosophy of Softness

Softness is not surrender to weakness.
It is surrender to truth.

Water is soft, yet it shapes stone.
A feather is light, yet it rides the wind with grace.
When you soften, you don't lose your strength;
you learn to move with life instead of against it.

Softness is how the soul breathes again after years of armour.
It is the moment the inner war ends.

You do not have to "become soft."
You are remembering you already were.
The world taught you to harden,
but your essence was always gentle.

Let that be enough.

Spiritual Meaning:

You are not learning softness;
you are remembering the peace that was always yours before fear entered.

The soft life is not about escape from the world.
It is about returning to your body as a safe place to live.
A home where breath is steady,
presence is possible,
and peace doesn't need permission.

Quote:

"A soft life begins when you stop abandoning yourself."

Healing Practice:

Tomorrow, when you feel the impulse to run from your own presence —
pause.
Place your hand on your chest.
Breathe once.
Stay with yourself for one moment longer than before.

That moment is where peace begins.

 ← THE RETRUN →

Chapter 15
HEALING IS NOT LINEAR

A return is not a failure.

A repeat is not a collapse.

It is your system showing you where love is still needed.

— Author

Healing is a paradox.

It moves forward by circling back.

It expands by revisiting what felt closed.

It transforms by bringing old pain into new awareness.

Many people believe healing should look clean, linear, organized —

as if you start broken and end healed,

like a straight path from darkness to light.

But the human heart does not move in straight lines.

It moves in spirals.

Healing circles.

It loops.

It revisits.

It unfolds in layers.
You return to the same wound again and again —
but each time with more capacity,
more breath,
more compassion,
more understanding of who you are now.
You are not falling back.
You are moving deeper in.

The Gentle Science of Returning
When an old pattern suddenly resurfaces —
the panic, the shutdown, the tight chest,
the racing thoughts, the numbness, the fear —
the first instinct is shame:
"Why is this happening again?"
"I thought I healed this."
"There must be something wrong with me."
But the truth is softer.
More loving.
More biological.
The nervous system does not choose what is "healthy."
It chooses what is familiar.
Your old pattern is a neural pathway you walked thousands of times.
It is wide, predictable, automatic —
like a highway carved by repetition.
Your new pattern — pausing, breathing, staying with yourself —
is a path you have only walked a few dozen times.
A beginner's trail.
Narrow. Tender. Still forming.
So when stress hits, your system does what systems do:
It takes the old highway.
This is not a failure.
This is efficiency.
This is the body doing what it learned to do to protect you.

Healing is simply the quiet devotion of choosing the new path
one more time than you choose the old one.
Not perfectly.
Not forever.
Just once more than before.
That is enough to rewire a life.

Why Patterns Return When You Least Expect Them
Trauma stored in the body does not leave because the mind has insight.
It leaves because the body feels safe enough to release it.
This means:
When the old wound returns,
it is not because you are weak.
It is because your system believes
you are finally strong enough
to meet the deeper layer.
A trigger is not a regression.
It is an invitation.
Your body whispers:
"I am ready to soften this now.
Stay with me."

Knowledge Changes the Mind. Practice Changes the Body.
Many people believe that once they understand their trauma —
their attachment style, their childhood patterns, the core wound —
the pain should dissolve.
But understanding is only the beginning.
The nervous system does not speak the language of concepts.
It speaks the language of repetition.
To your body, healing looks like:
pausing before reacting
breathing through discomfort
choosing presence instead of escape
feeling emotion instead of suppressing it

catching yourself a few seconds sooner
speaking gently to yourself after a mistake
These small choices seem insignificant,
but they are the building blocks of transformation.
Knowledge alone is like reading about swimming.
Practice is what teaches you how to float.

Mastery Is in the Basics

I think often about my Brazilian Jiu-Jitsu evenings in Balgowlah —
the familiar walk into the academy,
the sound of feet brushing the mats,
the soft hum of breath and effort,
the quiet dignity of learning something with your whole body.
On those nights, I feel both a beginner and a warrior.
Soft and strong.
Unsure and committed.
A student of movement, and a student of myself.

My coach, Murilo Amaral, a world champion, teaches in a way that has become a philosophy for my entire learning journey.
He never arrives on the mats as someone who has "achieved mastery."
He arrives as someone willing to meet the basics again,
as if the fundamentals themselves are alive,
full of secrets that only devotion can reveal.
It reminds me of George Leonard's book *Mastery*,
where he writes that real transformation is not found in flashes of brilliance
but in the slow, steady, patient return to the same practices
over and over,
with humility,
with presence,
with heart.
Murilo embodies this truth.
He doesn't rush technique.
He doesn't skip the foundational movements just because he is advanced.
He bows to the basics the way one bows to a teacher.

And somewhere along the way, I realized:
Healing works exactly the same way.
Healing is not the dramatic breakthrough.
It's not the one "a-ha" moment that changes your whole life.
It's not a single breathwork session,
a single journal entry,
a single therapy session.
Healing is the daily return.
It is the moment you pause instead of react.
The moment you breathe instead of abandoning yourself.
The moment you soften instead of collapse.
The moment you stay with the discomfort
a few seconds longer than the old version of you could.
These moments are tiny.
Almost invisible.
Quiet enough that nobody else will ever notice.
But they are everything.
Just like in BJJ,
you are not building perfection.
You are building capacity.
And capacity grows like roots —
slowly,
silently,
underground,
until one day you look back and realize:
You are no longer the person who breaks at the same place.
You are no longer the person who disappears inside the old pattern.
You are no longer the person who must fight themselves to survive the day.
Just like stepping onto the mats night after night,
you show up to your healing,
not as someone who is "finished,"
but as someone who is willing to begin again.
And that willingness —
that devotion —

is the true mastery.

The Spiral Path: What Looks Like Backwards Is Actually Forwards
Visualize a spiral staircase.
You circle around and find yourself facing the same view —
the same wound, the same fear, the same trigger —
but you are not on the same floor.
You are higher.
Wider.
More aware.
The wound has not returned to punish you.
It has returned to meet the version of you who can hold it now.
This is the difference:
Before:
You drowned inside the reaction.
Now:
You feel it,
you notice it,
you breathe,
you return.
That is healing.
Not the absence of the wound —
but the presence of your awareness.

The Plateau: Where the Real Transformation Happens
There will be long seasons where nothing seems to be changing.
Where you feel stuck.
Frozen.
Unmoving.
It feels like a failure,
but it is actually integration.
George Leonard called this "the plateau" —
the place where the body and mind reorganize themselves quietly,
under the surface,

while nothing seems to be happening.
The breakthrough happens later,
sudden and effortless,
but only because of the slow foundations laid before it.
You are not stuck.
You are becoming.
Even when nothing shows.

When the Old Reaction Happens Again
When you find yourself:
saying something you regret,
falling into old emotional loops,
feeling overwhelmed by a familiar fear,
shutting down instead of speaking,
chasing instead of pausing,
collapsing instead of grounding,
remember this:
You are no longer unconscious inside the pattern.
You are watching it.
You are noticing it.
You are awake.
Awareness is the first step of every transformation.
It is the moment the unconscious becomes conscious.
That alone is healing.

The Kindness That Changes Everything
Self-criticism keeps you stuck.
Self-compassion moves you forward.
When the old pattern returns, instead of saying:
"I'm pathetic."
"I'm still broken."
"I should be past this."
Try:
"This is familiar.

And I am learning."
"This is the old pathway.
And I can choose differently."
"This is a cycle.
And I am rising through it."
Healing does not ask you to be perfect.
It asks you to stay gentle.

The Spiritual Truth Beneath It All
You are not undoing your healing.
You are deepening it.
Every time the old wound rises,
it gives you a chance to meet it
with more presence,
more breath,
more softness
than you could before.
This is not regression.
This is awakening.

Spiritual Meaning:
You are not failing.
You are spiraling upward.
Each return brings you closer to freedom.
Quote:
"You are not going backwards.
You are returning —
to hold what was once too heavy
with hands that have grown stronger."
Healing Practice:
The next time the old pattern rises:
Pause.
Interrupt the automatic momentum.

Place a hand on your heart.
Bring your awareness into your body.
Say softly:
"This is familiar.
And I can choose differently now."
Choose differently once.
Not perfectly.
Just once more than before.
One gentle choice
is enough to change the direction of your entire life.

Chapter 16
YOU ARE BECOMING WHOLE

The quiet arrival.
"You are not healed when life never scares you.
You are healed when fear no longer decides who you are allowed to be."
— *Author*

Wholeness does not enter your life the way pain once did.
It does not burst through the door.
It does not announce itself.
It does not come with fireworks or declarations or any kind of triumph that the world can applaud.
  Wholeness arrives the way morning light touches a dark room —
softly, slowly, without permission, without force.
It appears in the smallest places first.
In breaths.
In pauses.
In the subtle warmth returning to your chest.
  It appears the first time you feel fear and do not run from yourself.

For most of our lives, fear has been the compass we unknowingly followed.
Fear of being abandoned.
Fear of being judged.
Fear of being misunderstood.
Fear of failing.
Fear of loving too much.
Fear of wanting too much.
Fear of not being enough.
Fear of being *too much*.

Fear shaped our choices so thoroughly that at some point,
We began mistaking fear for identity.

But fear is not who you are.
Fear is who you learned to be to survive.

When the wound begins to heal,
the world does not suddenly become safe —
you become the safety.

You begin to notice that fear is not a prophecy,
not a truth,
not a sign that something is wrong.
Fear is just energy moving through the body.
A wave.
A memory.
A whisper from an older moment saying:
"This once hurt me."

Fear is the echo,
not the present.

And yet, for most of your life, the echo controlled the entire symphony.

But slowly — almost imperceptibly — something begins to change.

You breathe.
You stay.
You feel your feet.
You come back to yourself.

Fear rises — and you do not obey it.

This is wholeness.

When Fear Stops Being the Authority

There will come a moment — quiet enough to miss if you're not paying attention —
when life tests you in the same way it always has,
but you respond differently.

A moment when someone raises their voice
and your chest does not collapse.

A moment when someone takes a step back
and your mind does not spiral into abandonment.

A moment when uncertainty arrives
and you do not panic or predict catastrophe.

A moment when silence appears
and you do not rush to fill it with apologies, explanations, or self-erasure.

A moment when someone loves you
and you do not shrink.

A moment when you love someone
and you do not disappear.

The moment is small —
so small that no one else would notice it.
But your soul does.
Your body does.
Your breath does.

It is the moment you realize:

Fear is no longer the one steering the ship.

Not gone.
Not defeated.
Just no longer the authority on your life.

You have become the one you listen to now.

The Fear That Lived Inside You Was Never a Monster — It Was a Child

When wholeness arrives, you begin to see fear differently.

Fear is not the enemy.
Fear is not the problem.
Fear is not something to conquer or eliminate.

Fear is a child of your past
still asking to be held.

The child who was overwhelmed.
The child who was shamed for needing help.
The child who was punished for crying.
The child who learned to perform strength.
The child who learned to hide softness.
The child who had no one to soothe them.
The child who absorbed the pain of adults who never healed themselves.

When fear rises in your chest today,
it is that child —
shaking, remembering, reaching for protection —
hoping someone finally knows what to do with them.

Wholeness arrives the moment
you become the one who knows.

The moment you say:
"I'm here.
I won't leave you.
You're safe with me now."

The moment you stop trying to silence fear
and begin to hold it with tenderness.

The moment you understand:

You were never alone inside yourself —
part of you was simply waiting for you to come back.

The Softening of the Fear of Death

Something else shifts too —
quietly, gently, naturally.

The fear of death begins to soften.

Not because you want to escape life.
Not because you seek endings.
Not because you have transcended human instinct.

The fear of death softens
because you are no longer afraid of *being here.*

Death is terrifying when you are abandoning yourself.
When your life is lived in fragments.
When your days are spent surviving instead of inhabiting.

But when you come home to yourself —
when you stop running —
when you stop trying to be someone else —
when you allow your life to matter,
to breathe,
to be touched by your own presence —

then death stops being a threat
and becomes a reminder:

"Live while you're here."

A person who is truly living
does not fear death
because they are not missing their life anymore.

Wholeness Is Not the End of Emotions

A common misunderstanding is that healing will turn you into someone who is always calm, always peaceful, always serene, always untouched.

But that is not healing —
that is dissociation dressed as enlightenment.

Wholeness does not numb you.
It returns you.

To your breath.
To your sensations.
To your instincts.
To your intuition.
To your heart.

Wholeness expands your capacity to feel,
not your ability to escape.

You still feel sadness,
but it no longer drowns you.

You still feel anger,
but it no longer controls you.

You still feel fear,
but it no longer dictates the terms of your life.

You still feel desire,
but it no longer turns into obsession or emptiness.

You still feel love,
but it no longer erases you.

Wholeness is not "no emotions."
Wholeness is full emotions with presence.

It is the ability to stand inside your waves
without losing yourself to the tide.

The Quiet Metrics of Becoming Whole

Wholeness is measured in quiet transformations, such as:

You trust your own pace.

You no longer apologize for existing.

You can sit alone without reaching for distraction.

Your body is no longer a battlefield.

You do not chase those who choose to walk away.

You no longer abandon yourself to keep the peace.

You no longer shrink to be loved.

You no longer perform to be chosen.

You no longer harden to survive the softness of others.

You forgive yourself faster.

You return to yourself sooner.

You no longer need chaos to feel alive.

You no longer confuse intensity with intimacy.

You no longer confuse calm with boredom.

You can feel joy without bracing for loss.

You can feel desire without shame.

You can feel love without fear.

Wholeness is not a moment —
it is a collection of moments
so gentle they often go unnoticed
until one day you realize:
　I am not who I was.
I am home.

When You Stop Abandoning Yourself, Your Life Becomes Your Own
　For years — maybe decades —
you lived in patterns that were never truly yours.
　People pleased you into invisibility.
Fear guided your choices.
Old wounds shaped your relationships.
Survival became your personality.
You wore masks so often you forgot the texture of your own face.
You lived on reflex rather than intention.
　But then, slowly...
beautifully...
inevitably...
　you began to return.

Your voice returned.
Your breath returned.
Your instincts returned.
Your boundaries returned.
Your softness returned.
Your power returned.
Your truth returned.
Your rhythm returned.

These returns are not loud.
They are not dramatic.
They do not impress the world.

But they awaken *you*.

And when you stop abandoning yourself —
your life becomes your own again.

The Spiritual Meaning of Wholeness

Wholeness is not becoming someone new.
Wholeness is remembering
who you were
before the world taught you to split yourself.

Before you were told to be small.
Before you were shamed for needing.
Before you were taught to fear your own softness.
Before your body became a battleground.
Before your heart learned to hide.
Before fear became your shepherd.
Before survival became your identity.

Wholeness is the reunion.

The returning.
The remembering.
The re-inhabiting.
The re-claiming.
The homecoming.

You become whole the moment you stop searching for your "true self"
and realize you have been carrying them inside you
all along —
quiet, patient, waiting.

The Body's Role in Becoming Whole

Your wholeness cannot be achieved through thought alone.

The mind can understand healing
long before the body is ready to live it.

Wholeness lives in:

your breath,

your nervous system,

your muscles,

your posture,

your digestion,

your boundaries,

your sleep,

your pace,

your slowness,

your presence.

Wholeness is the body finally believing
what the mind learned months or years ago:

"I am safe now."

This message does not arrive through words.
It arrives through repetition,

attention,

loving awareness,

and the simple daily choice
not to abandon yourself.

Wholeness is somatic —
it is felt, not thought.

The Moment You Know You're Whole

It will surprise you.

It will be an ordinary day.

You might be drinking tea.
Or resting on your bed.
Or speaking softly to yourself.
Or cooking.
Or watching light move across the wall.
And suddenly something inside you exhale
in a way it never has before.
Not a dramatic release.
Not a sobbing collapse.
Not a mystical opening.
Just a soft, simple knowing:
"I trust myself now."
Not because life became easier.
Not because pain disappeared.
Not because nothing scares you anymore.
But because you finally know:
You will not abandon yourself again.
That is wholeness.

What Wholeness Feels Like
It feels like a gentle spaciousness inside your ribs.
It feels like breathing without resistance.
It feels like belonging to yourself.
It feels like liking the person you are when no one is looking.
It feels like softness returning after years of armor.
It feels like trusting your own boundaries.
It feels like speaking honestly without shaking.
It feels like letting people leave without losing yourself.
It feels like letting people love you without shrinking.
It feels like being able to choose — truly choose.
It feels like ease, not safety.
It feels like freedom, not fearlessness.
It feels like home.

The Quiet Courage of Wholeness

Wholeness does not turn you into someone who never feels afraid.
Wholeness turns you into someone who can walk with fear
without collapsing, hiding, or losing your center.

You do not banish fear.
You accompany it.

You do not control the world.
You trust your response.

You do not eliminate uncertainty.
You develop the capacity to stay open inside it.

You do not become invincible.
You become available —
to life, to love, to possibility, to yourself.

Wholeness is courage wrapped in softness.

The Final Understanding:

You are not here to avoid endings.
You are here to live fully in the moments that exist.
You are here to let life touch you.
You are here to feel the full expression of being human.
You are here to return to yourself again and again
until returning becomes staying.

You are whole
not because you no longer break
but because you now know how to hold yourself
every time you do.

Quote:
"You do not lose fear by fighting it.
You lose fear by coming home to the one who felt afraid."

Healing Practice:

When fear rises, do not ask, *"How do I stop this?"*
Ask softly:
"Can I stay with myself while this moves through?"

YOU ARE BECOMING WHOLE

If the answer is yes —
even for one breath,
even for one second —
you are already whole.

Chapter 17
Returning to Innocence: Aging as a Sacred Homecoming

The Circle Completes Itself

Human life is not a straight line.
It's a circle.

We come into this world helpless—soft, open, defenseless, needing everything.
And if we live long enough, we return to that same softness at the end.

This is not failure.
This is grace.

We are not losing ourselves as we age.
We are finding ourselves again.

Finding the original self—before the world taught us to armor up, to push through, to never show weakness.
Finding the softness we were born with.
Finding our way back to innocence.

When the Body Becomes Tender Again

As the body weakens with age, something beautiful happens underneath:
The soul becomes more visible.

All the striving to prove yourself—it starts to quiet.
All the walls you spent decades building—they begin to soften, gently.
All the masks you wore just to survive—they don't fit anymore.

The elder becomes more sensitive.
More easily moved to tears or laughter.
Less defended against the world.
More present in each moment.
Less attached to how things should be.

This is not weakness.
This is what strength becomes when it no longer needs to prove itself.

The body may be frail, but the spirit grows vast.
The hands may tremble, but the heart opens wider.
The steps may slow, but the presence deepens.

Why Our Elders Live in Yesterday

There's a gentle reason older people talk more about the past than the future.

It's not that they're stuck or can't move forward.
It's that the past is where the harvest is.

Think of it like this:

When you're young, you're planting seeds—working, building, rushing toward tomorrow.
When you're old, you're walking through the garden—looking at what grew, understanding what it all meant.

The elderly brain shifts from remembering tiny details to remembering what mattered.

They might not recall what time the party started or what someone wore.
But they remember how it felt to be loved, to be hurt, to be truly alive.

Their brain is doing something sacred:

It's turning a lifetime into wisdom.
It's distilling all those years into meaning.
It's gathering the lessons so they can be passed down.

The stories they tell over and over?
Those aren't just memories.
Those are the parts of their life that shaped their soul.

And when they speak about the past with tears in their eyes or joy on their face—
they're not lost in nostalgia.
They're teaching you what matters.

A Message for Your Future Self

Here's something important to understand now, while you're reading this:
You will be old someday.

Your body will soften.
Your hair will turn gray.
Your hands will carry the marks of all these years.

And when that day comes, you'll walk back through your life—
through all the moments, all the choices, all the pain and joy—
and you'll want it to be a garden you can rest in.

This is why healing matters now.

If you bury your pain today,
if you push it down and step over it,
if you leave it unprocessed in the basement of your heart—

It will still be there when you're old.

But then you'll be sitting in a garden full of weeds you don't have the strength to pull anymore.

The wounds you didn't tend to will become the stories that keep you up at night.
The apologies you never made will become the regrets that follow you.
The love you were too afraid to accept will become the longing that aches in your chest.

But if you do the work now—

If you feel your feelings instead of avoiding them.
If you speak your truth instead of swallowing it.
If you forgive—yourself and others—while you still can.
If you let yourself be loved, even when it's scary.

Then when you're old, you'll sit in a garden that's soft and beautiful.

A place of peace.
A place where you can finally rest.
A place you're proud to have grown.

Your elder self is already inside you, watching.

What kind of garden are you planting for them?

The Return of the Inner Child

There's a sacred pattern in how we age:

When you become a parent, your child becomes your mirror—showing you everything you haven't healed yet.

But when you grow old, your inner child becomes your mirror again.

The elder often returns to childlike ways:

Wonder at small things (a bird, a flower, the warmth of sun)

Tears that come easily, laughter that bubbles up freely

Needing to be cared for, held, comforted

Living right here, right now—not worried about tomorrow

Saying what they feel without caring what others think

This isn't senility.
This is the soul coming home.

All the parts of yourself you had to hide when you were growing up—
the playful one,
the tender one,
the one who needed help,
the one who just wanted to be held—

They return at the end.

And if you've done your healing, this return is not scary.
It's a relief.
It's finally being allowed to be fully yourself.

The Holiness of Needing Help

Our world teaches us that independence is everything.

Stand on your own.
Don't be a burden.

Never show weakness.
Never need anyone.
> But the elder teaches us something different.
> Needing help is not shameful.

Asking for care is not a weakness.
Softness at the end of life is the purest form of wisdom.
> The elder who can say "I need you" without apologizing,

who can let someone feed them, bathe them, hold them without feeling less than—
> That elder is teaching us how to be human.
> Because we all started completely helpless.

And we all end up needing help again.
> *The circle is sacred.*
> Between birth and death, we spend so much time trying to be strong, independent,

unbreakable.
But the bookends of life whisper the truth:
> We were made to need each other.

We were made to be tender.
We were made to be held

What Falls Away, What Remains

Aging strips away everything that isn't real.

The elderly let go of:

Status and what people think

The need to achieve and prove

Collecting more things

Planning five years ahead

Being right all the time

Looking a certain way

What stays is:

The people they love

Simple joys (warm tea, a kind word, a sunset)

Being present

Gratitude for small things

Just **being** instead of always doing

The elder is not losing who they are.

The elder is finding who they've always been underneath all the roles.

Beneath "mother," beneath "professional," beneath all the identities—there's just **a soul.**

And that soul becomes clearer as the body becomes quieter.

The Spiritual Truth of Aging

In every spiritual tradition, aging is seen as preparation for the ultimate letting go.

The Buddhist teaching:

Aging is your daily reminder that nothing lasts. Your own body shows you: everything changes, everything passes. This prepares you for the final release—death itself. The elder becomes a living meditation on impermanence.

The Hindu teaching:

Life has four stages. The last stage is called *Sannyasa*—renunciation. You let go of worldly attachments to focus on the spiritual. Elders naturally move into this, even if they don't call it that. They care less about the world and more about the soul.

The Christian mystical teaching:

Jesus said, "Unless you become like little children, you will never enter heaven." The elder circles back to this innocence. Aging is becoming like a child again—open, trusting, dependent on grace.

The Indigenous teaching:

Elders are the wisdom keepers. They don't need to do anything anymore. Their job is to be—to hold the stories, to carry the teachings, to remind everyone what actually matters.

In every tradition, the message is the same:

Aging is not an ending. It's a return to the beginning—closer to God, closer to truth, closer to home.

The Gift the Elderly Give Us

Every elder you meet is teaching you something, whether they know it or not.

They show us:

You can lose strength and still have power.

You can need help and still have dignity.

You can forget things and still remember love.
You can slow down and still matter.
You can be soft and still be whole.

They remind us:

Life is short.

People are what matter.

Kindness is everything.

Bodies are temporary.

Love is what's real.

They prepare us:

For our own aging.

For our own letting go.

For our own return to softness.

When you sit with an elder—really sit, really listen, hold their hand—you're receiving something sacred.

They're showing you how to age with grace.

They're teaching you how to release what doesn't matter.

They're walking the path you'll walk someday.

Pay attention.

In the Garden: Meeting Your Younger Self

Close your eyes for a moment.

Imagine you're old now.

Your body is soft. Your hair is silver. Your hands tell the story of a whole life lived.

You're sitting in a garden—quiet, warm, peaceful.

And there, across from you, sits your younger self.

The one who's reading this right now.

The one who's carrying so much.

The one who's trying so hard.

The one who's afraid they're not enough.

The one who thinks love has to be earned.

The one who's holding pain they don't know how to release.

What would you tell them?

Maybe you'd say:

"It's okay to slow down. You don't have to prove anything."

"You are already enough. You always were."

"The people who really love you will stay. Stop trying to earn it."

"Those wounds—feel them now. Don't bury them. They don't go away, they just wait."

"It's not weak to need help. It's human."

"Let yourself be soft. The world won't break you."

"What you think is so important now—most of it won't matter. Love matters. Presence matters. That's it."

What wisdom would flow from your elder heart to your younger, striving self?

Here's the beautiful truth:

You don't have to wait until you're old to receive this wisdom.

That elder version of you already exists inside you.

That knowing is available right now.

Every time you choose rest over rush.

Every time you ask for help instead of struggling alone.

Every time you let yourself feel instead of pushing it down.

Every time you choose truth over performance.

You're becoming the elder you want to be.

You're planting seeds in a garden you'll walk through someday.

The Sacred Preparation

Aging is not punishment for living too long.

Aging is the soul getting ready to go home.

The body weakens so the spirit can be seen.

The ego melts so the true self can emerge.

The past becomes vivid so the lessons can be gathered.

The future becomes less important so the present can be fully lived.

And when the very end comes—

when the breath slows and softens,

when the body is ready to release,

when the soul steps out of form—

The elder is not afraid.

Because they've been practicing this letting go their whole life.
Every goodbye prepared them.
Every loss taught them.
Every time they softened, they became more ready.
They return to the innocence they started with.
No longer afraid.
No longer defending.
No longer needing to prove anything.
Just *being*.
Just *breathing*.
Just **resting** in what has always been true:
You are loved.
You belong.
You always have.
You always will.

The Wisdom the Elderly Carry
If you listen closely, every elder is saying the same thing in different words:
Life is a circle.
You don't move away from innocence.
You spiral back to it.
All the pain, all the healing, all the years—
it's all bringing you back to the softness you were born with.
And when you're old, looking back over it all—
you'll see clearly.
The pain that broke you open.
The love that held you together.
The moments that actually mattered.
The people who stayed.
And you'll understand:
Nothing was wasted.
Every step, every tear, every joy—
all of it brought you here.

To this quiet place.
To this soft heart.
To this sacred return to yourself.
This is the gift of growing old.
Not loss.
Not decay.
Not the end.
But **the return.**
The homecoming.
The closing of the circle.
The sacred arrival back at innocence—
Where you always belonged.

Tend Your Garden Now
So here's the invitation as you're reading this:
Don't wait until you're old to start healing.
Don't wait until your body is frail to soften your heart.
Don't wait until the end to understand what matters.
Do the work now.
Feel what needs to be felt.
Say what needs to be said.
Love who needs to be loved.
Forgive what needs to be forgiven.
Release what needs to be released.
Because someday—
and that day will come—
You'll be the elder.
You'll look back at this moment.
And you'll either see a garden that bloomed from your courage—
Or you'll see the pain you left buried, still waiting to be held.
The choice is yours.
Plant beauty now.
Water it with truth.
Tend it with love.

So that when you're old and tired and ready to rest—
you can sit in the garden of your life and smile.

Not because it was perfect.

But because it was **yours.**

Because you **lived it.**

Because you **felt it.**

Because you didn't run from yourself.

That's the promise of conscious aging.

A garden you can rest in.

A life you can be proud of.

A heart that's finally, completely, peacefully—

Home.

Epilogue — The Gentle Doorway

Death is the one truth every human carries quietly inside them, like a note folded in the pocket of the soul.
We do not speak of it often, yet it shapes our fears, our choices, our longings, our urgency to love and be loved.
And yet—death is not the monster we imagine.
Death is not the great darkness.
Death is a doorway.

When the body approaches the end, science tells us something beautiful happens: the brain begins to release its grip.
Neurons fire more slowly, the mind softens into a dreamlike state, and the boundaries of self loosen.
The default mode network—the part of the brain that creates "I, me, mine"—quietly dissolves, just as it does in deep meditation, psychedelic states, or moments of profound awakening.

In the final hours, the body shuts down in a specific sequence: breath slows, oxygen decreases, and the brain gently shifts into what researchers call "burst patterns," waves of electrical activity that resemble the dreaming mind.
Many scientists believe this is the brain's natural way of protecting us—softening awareness, cushioning fear, allowing the mind to float.

It is not chaos.
It is choreography.
A soft landing arranged by nature itself.

Hospice nurses often say the same thing:
that the moment of passing is peaceful, quiet, like exhaling after holding breath for too long.
People speak to loved ones who are not in the room.
They see light, gardens, oceans, ancestors.
They smile.
They soften.
They return.

No matter what we believe about the afterlife, something becomes undeniably clear in these final moments:

Death is not an ending—it is a transition.

Spiritual traditions across the world describe it the same way:

The Buddhists call it *the great return.*
The Hindus call it *the shedding of the temporary body.*
The Sufis call it *the homecoming of the soul.*
The Mystics call it *the dissolving into God.*
Indigenous elders call it *the crossing of the river.*

And children—those wise beings closest to both entrances—describe it simply: "Going back to the light."

Death is not meant to be feared.
Death is meant to be understood.

We fear death because we fear losing the self we worked so hard to build.
We fear the unknown.
We fear the dark.

But the truth is softer:

Death is not the dark.
Death is the letting go of the tightness that kept us from seeing how bright we already were.

The body may fall away, but what you discovered in these pages—
your awareness,
your tenderness,

your presence,
your capacity to stay with yourself—
those are not limited to the body.

You have touched the part of yourself that does not end.

And so when the final moment one day arrives—not now, not soon, but whenever life has finished its teaching—
you will not face a void.
You will face a return.

A return to the softness you were born with.
A return to the vastness you glimpsed in moments of awakening.
A return to the love that shaped you long before you had a name.
A return to the place inside you that never suffered, never feared, never broke.

Death is not a punishment.
Death is a release.
A liberation.
A quiet merging back into what you always were beneath the stories, the wounds, the body, the time you were given.

If life is the inhale,
then death is simply the exhale.
The soft falling back into the arms that held you from the beginning.

And perhaps the greatest secret is this:

You do not have to wait until your final breath to feel this peace.
Every time you let go of an old identity,
every time you soften instead of harden,
every time you return to yourself after abandoning yourself—
you practice dying without fear.

You practice meeting the unknown with grace.
You practice releasing the small self and resting in something larger.
You practice the homecoming.

In this way, living becomes the preparation,
and dying becomes the gentle completion.

Not an ending.
A returning.

A circle closing.
A soul finally resting in its own light.
    Thank you for walking this path.
Thank you for your courage, your softness, your willingness to meet yourself honestly.
Thank you for choosing healing in a world that forgets how sacred becoming whole truly is.
    May your life be full.
May your heart be steady.
May your soul remember.
    And when the time comes—
may your return be peaceful,
beautiful,
and filled with the light you carried all along.

www.ingramcontent.com/pod-product-compliance
Lightning Source LLC
Chambersburg PA
CBHW061208070526
44583CB00025B/3157